Current
CONTROVERSIES

| Freedom of the Press

Other Books in the Current Controversies Series

Current
CONTROVERSIES

Freedom of the Press

Andrew Karpan, Book Editor

GREENHAVEN
PUBLISHING

Published in 2020 by Greenhaven Publishing, LLC
353 3rd Avenue, Suite 255, New York, NY 10010

Cover image: Stock image/Shutterstock.com

Library of Congress Cataloging-in-Publication Data

Names: Karpan, Andrew, editor.
Title: Freedom of the press / Andrew Karpan, book editor.
Description: New York : Greenhaven Publishing, 2020. | Series: Current controversies
| Includes bibliographical references and index. | Audience: Grades 9–12.
Identifiers: LCCN 2019022813 | ISBN 9781534506053 (library
binding) | ISBN 9781534506046 (paperback)
Subjects: LCSH: Freedom of the press—United States.
Classification: LCC KF4774 .F743 2020 | DDC 323.44/50973—dc23
LC record available at https://lccn.loc.gov/2019022813

Manufactured in the United States of America

Website: http://greenhavenpublishing.com

Contents

Chapter 1: Is a Digital Press a Freer Press?

Pew Research Center

In 2006, a collection of editors, professors, and media researchers met to discuss the future of a free press in a time when sinking ad revenues and subscriptions were beginning to make newspapers financially unsustainable. They turn to the internet as media's future.

Yes: Digital Journalism Allows News to Reach More People, Creating a More Educated Public

Damian Radcliffe

In 2017, writers from a small newspaper called the *Storm Lake Times* won the Pulitzer Prize for Editorial Writing, beating out nominees from the *Washington Post* and the *Houston Chronicle*. In a time when national headlines debate "fake news," Radcliffe points out that some of the best journalism today is being done on a local level, where publications can take advantage of the lower overhead of digital journalism and can reflect the direct, everyday concerns of their readers.

Stuart Dredge

The "breaking news" model of reporting, invented by ABC News' coverage of the Iran hostage crisis in 1979–1981 and popularized by channels like CNN and Fox News, created a press that valued a narrow kind of news story. New and exclusively digital publications like *Vice News* and *BuzzFeed News* have blazed their own path by reporting from parts of the world that wouldn't have an audience on TV news decades ago.

Katerina Eva Matsa and Elisa Shearer

A little over two-thirds of Americans consume news through social media, and most say that the convenience and ease of access outweigh their concerns over accuracy or quality. If anything, readers of digital journalism are better equipped to find the human biases that have always been implicit in reporting because of how many opposing viewpoints are available at the click of a button.

No: Digital Journalism Has Reduced the Number of Journalists Working Today and Generates Less Accurate News Coverage

Digital journalism may be able to reach more people, but that hasn't translated to better quality journalism. In fact, the increased pressure of the digital news cycle to quickly churn out articles has made journalists more prone to mistakes, as they're expected to work longer hours and work on a diverse range of digital projects simultaneously.

The shuttering of the *St. Marys Journal Argus*, a local newspaper in the town of St. Marys, Ontario, is a case study in the inability of small newspapers to adapt to the digital climate. Beyond writers losing their jobs, it also causes communities to lose their voices and their ability to knowledgeably participate in a democratic society.

Newspapers aren't just disappearing. Newsrooms are shrinking, the largest publishers are vast advertising empires, and stories come self-reported and are only verified long after the fact. It's a system that lavishly rewards the companies that know how to play it, but it does little to inform the public.

Chapter 2: Does Media Conglomeration Censor the Press?

In the late 1990s, the FTC began allowing single media companies to control bigger swathes of the marketplace—an effort that left less and less room for smaller companies to offer alternatives to mainstream news coverage, argues Ted Turner, a media executive who once ran a small Atlanta-based network that eventually became CNN. With many of the independent businesses in the media industry gone, Turner asks, where will new ideas come from?

Yes: Media Conglomeration Has a Chilling Effect on Free Journalistic Expression

Michael Corcoran

Media plays an essential role in American politics: it is the forum where the majority of voters become informed about who is running for office and what they stand for. By allowing the media industry to be run by fewer and fewer companies, we allow our democracy to be managed by an increasingly smaller cabal of corporate interests.

Glenn Greenwald

When the White House wanted to make sure major news channels devoted coverage to a presidential speech in 2009, it called the CEOs of Disney and GE, the electronics giant that bought NBC in 2004. It wasn't hard to ask this favor: that year, GE spent more money lobbying Congress and the president than any company except the oil giant Chevron. GE's control of the NBC newsroom is even more chilling, as Greenwald reports that it ordered one of its news programs to halt coverage of competitor Fox News, which had begun running negative coverage of GE in order to force the company's hand.

Mike Floorwalker

Media conglomeration has also produced worse news coverage that is informed by fewer people. Because those same individuals enjoy outsized influence in the American political system, the effect is not unlike that of government censorship.

No: Media Conglomeration Can Keep a Free Press Alive

Kyle Pope

Since being taken over by Amazon, one of the biggest companies in the world, the *Washington Post* has won the Pulitzer Prize and largely expanded its online footprint, publishing more articles per day than the *New York Times*. Corporate ownership, rather than stifling the voices of its journalists, gives them the freedom to chase stories and improves access in ways that most newsrooms lack the resources to facilitate.

Dan Kennedy
Corporations can value a free press as much as ordinary citizens. Also citing Amazon's ownership of the *Washington Post*, Kennedy points to the value Amazon's Jeff Bezos places on the civic importance of the newspaper and Amazon's willingness to expand the reach of its journalistic efforts. A free press doesn't necessarily need to pit companies against reporters.

Chapter 3: Does Litigation Hamper a Free Press?

Electronic Frontier Foundation
Examples of overt suppression of free speech are hard to find in the US, but libel laws give the subjects of press coverage the chance to legally challenge that coverage if parts of it could be considered either false or merely speculative. Ultimately, even if the statements aren't found libelous, it is often expensive for media companies to defend themselves, adding another potential financial expense to a free press.

Yes: Libel Suits Are a Form of Censorship

Derek Wilding
Using the example of Australia's New South Wales, Wilding looks at how libel laws have encouraged suits over blog and social media posts and how the laws themselves aren't equipped for primarily digital publishing. While the number of libel suits has risen, few are actually won, creating an expensive legal quagmire for both parties involved.

Jeffrey A. Tucker
When widely enforced, the effect of libel laws is to "chill" a free press, meaning to frighten journalists away from reporting stories. For

much of the past half-century, the Supreme Court case *The New York Times vs. Sullivan* established that simple journalistic mistakes do not count as libel and that actual malice had to be proven in order to send a case to court. But, Tucker warns, those protections are only as strong as the current laws are.

No: Privacy Is As Important As a Free Press

Paul Sturges

Freedom of expression in a society—by an individual or by an organ of the press—comes with responsibilities of citizenry, such as the larger security of that society or the public safety of those who live in it. Libel laws exist to ensure the enforcement of these responsibilities.

David Engel

The press largely creates the reputation of public figures, and these figures have the right to not have this damaged without just cause. Most libel suits are, in fact, not about money at all: as Engel notes, they are often settled with an apology and a retraction of the incorrectly reported fact. In that regard, these cases are valuable tools for protecting individuals from the power of the press.

Chapter 4: Is Public Funding Good for a Free Press?

The Shorenstein Center

Beginning in 2011, residents of Flint, Michigan, began reporting unsafe drinking water, but few journalists from major news agencies were interested in taking on a story so far away from their own homes. In its stead, a nonprofit called the Ford Foundation stepped in, hiring an investigative reporter who—with the help of a branch of the ACLU—uncovered a national scandal.

Yes: Public Funding Is the Only Way Journalism Can Survive

Andrew Dodd

There is abundant evidence that the free market is failing the larger public in providing the kind of journalistic reporting a democracy needs to function. In addition to long-standing traditions of government-funded news channels, Dodd calls for the funding of newspapers and news websites, too. Additionally, with small grants, the government has the ability to open the doors to reporters who wouldn't be published elsewhere.

Ilma Ibrisevic

By relying on tax-deductible charitable funding, journalistic nonprofits are unburdened from having to satisfy owners with ad revenue, giving them the editorial and creative independence that few media organizations enjoy. They fill a vital gap in between the narrowing range of what mainstream media covers and the necessity of an informed public.

No: Government Funding Will Only Make the Press Less Free

Bill Wirtz

Marketplaces provide a diversity of choices and let readers choose which ones best match their interests. When the media landscape changes, that change should be directed by the needs and desires of the readers, not what the government deems necessary.

Tim Luckhurst

The independence of journalists from the interference of the state is a vital aspect of a democratic society; often it is the press that holds politicians accountable to the public. Permitting the government to fund journalists would permit them to regulate them and undermine this social contract.

Foreword

C ontroversy" is a word that has an undeniably unpleasant connotation. It carries a definite negative charge. Controversy can spoil family gatherings, spread a chill around classroom and campus discussion, inflame public discourse, open raw civic wounds, and lead to the ouster of public officials. We often feel that controversy is almost akin to bad manners, a rude and shocking eruption of that which must not be spoken or thought of in polite, tightly guarded society. To avoid controversy, to quell controversy, is often seen as a public good, a victory for etiquette, perhaps even a moral or ethical imperative.

Yet the studious, deliberate avoidance of controversy is also a whitewashing, a denial, a death threat to democracy. It is a false sterilizing and sanitizing and superficial ordering of the messy, ragged, chaotic, at times ugly processes by which a healthy democracy identifies and confronts challenges, engages in passionate debate about appropriate approaches and solutions, and arrives at something like a consensus and a broadly accepted and supported way forward. Controversy is the megaphone, the speaker's corner, the public square through which the citizenry finds and uses its voice. Controversy is the life's blood of our democracy and absolutely essential to the vibrant health of our society.

Our present age is certainly no stranger to controversy. We are consumed by fierce debates about technology, privacy, political correctness, poverty, violence, crime and policing, guns, immigration, civil and human rights, terrorism, militarism, environmental protection, and gender and racial equality. Loudly competing voices are raised every day, shouting opposing opinions, putting forth competing agendas, and summoning starkly different visions of a utopian or dystopian future. Often these voices attempt to shout the others down; there is precious little listening and considering among the cacophonous din. Yet listening and considering, too, are essential to the health of a democracy. If controversy is democracy's lusty lifeblood, respectful listening and careful thought are its higher faculties, its brain, its conscience.

Current Controversies does not shy away from or attempt to hush the loudly competing voices. It seeks to provide readers with as wide and representative as possible a range of articulate voices on any given controversy of the day, separates each one out to allow it to be heard clearly and fairly, and encourages careful listening to each of these well-crafted, thoughtfully expressed opinions, supplied by some of today's leading academics, thinkers, analysts, politicians, policy makers, economists, activists, change agents, and advocates. Only after listening to a wide range of opinions on an issue, evaluating the strengths and weaknesses of each argument, assessing how well the facts and available evidence mesh with the stated opinions and conclusions, and thoughtfully and critically examining one's own beliefs and conscience can the reader begin to arrive at his or her own conclusions and articulate his or her own stance on the spotlighted controversy.

This process is facilitated and supported in each Current Controversies volume by an introduction and chapter overviews that provide readers with the essential context they need to begin engaging with the spotlighted controversies, with the debates surrounding them, and with their own perhaps shifting or nascent opinions on them. Chapters are organized around several key questions that are answered with diverse opinions representing all points on the political spectrum. In its content, organization, and methodology, readers are encouraged to determine the authors' point of view and purpose, interrogate and analyze the various arguments and their rhetoric and structure, evaluate the arguments' strengths and weaknesses, test their claims against available facts and evidence, judge the validity of the reasoning, and bring into clearer, sharper focus the reader's own beliefs and conclusions and how they may differ from or align with those in the collection or those of classmates.

Research has shown that reading comprehension skills improve dramatically when students are provided with compelling, intriguing, and relevant "discussable" texts. The subject matter of these collections could not be more compelling, intriguing, or urgently relevant to today's students and the world they are poised to inherit. The anthologized articles also provide the basis for stimulating, lively, and passionate classroom debates. Students who are compelled to anticipate objections to their own argument and identify the flaws in those of an opponent read more carefully, think more critically, and steep themselves in relevant context, facts, and information more thoroughly. In short, using discussable text of the kind provided by every single volume in the Current Controversies series encourages close reading, facilitates reading comprehension, fosters research, strengthens critical thinking, and greatly enlivens and energizes classroom discussion and participation. The entire learning process is deepened, extended, and strengthened.

If we are to foster a knowledgeable, responsible, active, and engaged citizenry, we must provide readers with the intellectual, interpretive, and critical-thinking tools and experience necessary to make sense of the world around them and of the all-important debates and arguments that inform it. We must encourage them not to run away from or attempt to quell controversy but to embrace it in a responsible, conscientious, and thoughtful way, to sharpen and strengthen their own informed opinions by listening to and critically analyzing those of others. This series encourages respectful engagement with and analysis of current controversies and competing opinions and fosters a resulting increase in the strength and rigor of one's own opinions and stances. As such, it helps readers assume their rightful place in the public square and provides them with the skills necessary to uphold their awesome responsibility—guaranteeing the continued and future health of a vital, vibrant, and free democracy.

Introduction

> *"My goal was to be an honest broker*
> *of information"*
>
> > -Dan Rather, American
> > journalist

In September of 2018, the journalism watchdog group Muck Rack reported that according to US Department of Labor data there were over six public relations professionals for every one journalist.[1] This was an increase from 2016, when there were five, a figure that was itself double that of 2006. The data suggests at least two things: there are fewer journalists today, but there are just as many people who want to shape how we think.

In a democratic society, outright despots rarely present a challenge to a free press. Even the hazy, secretive maze of government can be illuminated. Freedom of Information Act requests can be submitted and litigated—for instance, even FBI files can be requested and entered into the public record once an investigation is no longer active.[2] Spies can be arrested, but the journalists who publish their findings walk scot-free, like Glen Greenwald, who won the Pulitzer Prize in 2014 for publishing documents leaked to him by former CIA employee Edward Snowden. The threats to a free press are, instead, practical ones. Journalists, as Muck Rack's analysis suggests, are increasingly outnumbered by those who would rather tell them what they should report.

The replacement of newspapers with social media[3] and the creation of enormous media companies has reduced the sheer number of journalists employed in newsrooms.[4] In their place come public relations professionals, eager to fill that vacancy with their own versions of the world. Also in their place come ordinary citizens who craft stories with their cell phones. There may be fewer and fewer paid journalists, but there are millions more volunteers who follow the whim of what they feel is important.

Nonetheless, the knee-jerk reaction to large media companies is to oppose them, but there remains the argument that Amazon— the single largest online business in the world—has both kept alive and improved one of America's important newspapers, the *Washington Post*. Additionally, many of the ills of today's press cannot be blamed on the internet. Large media companies were the product of the capital-heavy twenty-four-hour news cycle and the deregulation of the airwaves, which came in the form of the Telecommunications Act of 1996. This allowed single companies to own larger percentages of the media marketplace. If anything, the internet has allowed that hegemony to be broken. In a nation of citizen journalists, it is easier than ever for one's voice to find a platform.

But even a successful digital news website can find itself forcibly muted. In 2016, the popular news site Gawker entered bankruptcy and was forced to shutter its doors as a result of a privacy lawsuit filed by Hulk Hogan, a subject of one of the site's more lurid stories. If it isn't the feared political dictator breaking the people's proverbial printing press, then it is a thousand people who use the legal system to enforce their sense of what the world should know. But should individuals have no recourse to defend their reputations? Should we let the press rule our imaginations unchecked?

Because a free press is considered to be a self-evident right of a free people, journalists can be said to perform a necessary public service. This is why journalism is often subsidized with public funding. In the United States, this occurs largely through the nonprofit infrastructure in which companies can subsist entirely on donations, which are deducted from the tax payments of donors. It can also be directly funded, as is the case with the Corporation for Public Broadcasting, which is governed by a nine-member board of directors selected by the president and partially funds news networks like PBS and NPR. With the security and backing of the public, they provide a model free from many of the recent challenges limiting journalists today. However, some argue that they also provide a way for governments to reign in the press they fund, preventing it from being truly free. In 2005, the Corporation for Public Broadcasting was accused of hiring a consultant with "conservative ties" to analyze the politics of characters appearing on a number of PBS and NPR news shows, a move that allegedly targeted critics of the Iraq War.[5] A press that is given reason to fear critical political coverage is not a free one.

These debates animate the place that the news holds in our collective imagination. Knowing what is happening in the world is the default needed to take action in it. Journalists are far from the only people paid to shape our worldviews, but they represent the people we have collectively decided should be shaping it. The debates contained in *Current Controversies: Freedom of the Press* demonstrate just how important that position is.

Notes

[1] Mike Schneider, "There are now more than 6 PR pros for every journalist," Muck Rack. https://muckrack.com/blog/2018/09/06/there-are-now-more-than-6-pr-pros-for-every-journalist

[2] The Freedom of Information Act requires the full or redacted disclosure of unreleased government documents upon request. If not given, journalists can, and often do, sue the federal government in order to force the release.

[3] Elisa Shearer, "Social media outpaces print newspapers in the U.S. as a news source," Pew Research Center. https://www.pewresearch.org/fact-tank/2018/12/10/social-media-outpaces-print-newspapers-in-the-u-s-as-a-news-source/

[4] Elizabeth Grieco, "Newsroom employment dropped nearly a quarter in less than 10 years, with greatest decline at newspapers," Pew Research Center. https://www.pewresearch.org/fact-tank/2018/07/30/newsroom-employment-dropped-nearly-a-quarter-in-less-than-10-years-with-greatest-decline-at-newspapers/

[5] David Folkenflik, "CPB Memos Indicate Level of Monitoring," NPR. https://www.npr.org/templates/story/story.php?storyId=4724317

CHAPTER 1

Is a Digital Press a Freer Press?

The Decline of the Printing Press, the Rise of the Digital Press

Pew Research Center

The Pew Research Center is a project of the Pew Charitable Trusts. The Center acts as a nonpartisan research organization and is well known for its widely cited public opinion polling.

The threat to newspapers now appears from nearly every indicator. From 1950 through 1999, for instance, newspaper revenue grew seven percent a year. From 2000 through 2006, by contrast, it has grown by just 0.5%. Then in the first quarter of 2006, growth was even less: 0.35%.

And though online ad revenues continue to soar, they currently account for just five percent of all newspaper company revenue. In addition to sluggish ad growth, newspapers are challenged with circulation declines, a skeptical Wall Street, ownership changes—such as Knight Ridder's recent sale of its 32 papers—and perhaps most notably, adapting to the world of online news.

In this, the third of our roundtables on the future of the news media, six experts from inside the newspaper industry discuss its future, its fate, and the changes it must make to survive. They are:

- **Phil Meyer**, Knight Chair in Journalism, School of Journalism and Mass Communication at the University of North Carolina;
- **John Carroll**, editor of the Los Angeles Times from 2000 to 2005;
- **Rick Edmonds**, Researcher and Writer for the Poynter Institute and co-author of the newspaper chapter for the State of the News Media Annual Report;

"Challenges to the Newspaper Industry," Pew Research Center, Washington, DC (July 24, 2006). http://www.journalism.org/2006/07/24/challenges-to-the-newspaper-industry/. Used in accordance with Pew Research Center reuse Policy. http://www.pewresearch.org/terms-and-conditions/. Usage in no way implies endorsement.

- **Paul Ginocchio**, Media Analyst for Deutsche Bank. In 2005, Paul won a "Best on the Street" stock pricing award from the Wall Street Journal.
- **Lou Ureneck**, Chairman of the Department of Journalism at Boston University. Before his academic career, Ureneck serves as the deputy managing editor for the Philadelphia Inquirer and spent 22 years at the Portland Press Herald.
- **Rick Rodriguez**, Executive Editor and Senior Vice President of The Sacramento Bee, and in 2005-2006, President of the American Society of Newspaper Editors.

1. How much confidence do you have that traditional mainstream media organizations will survive and thrive in the transition to the Internet?

Paul Ginocchio: I have 100% confidence that the mainstream media organizations will survive. The toughest issue will be the transition period (from print to online, broadcast to broadband), but once the migration is over, cheaper distribution costs should enable media companies to more than fund the news gathering resources. The total cost of editorial for most newspapers is only 15% of sales, so current editorial resources can survive on a much lower revenue base.

Rick Edmonds: High. They have what democracy needs and it has market value too—original reporting and professional editing and packaging. I don't see that emerging elsewhere as yet. But the economic transition will be long and tough.

Phil Meyer: Very little. The most successful applications of the Internet are likely to come from unexpected sources, as Craig Newmark has so clearly demonstrated. Traditional media organizations are risk averse and unwilling to invest enough in new experiments.

John Carroll: Some will survive and some will thrive, but there are real questions about the quantity and quality of original journalism that will be produced. We may well look back on the last forty years and view them as an anomaly, in which newspapers enjoyed such monopolistic conditions that they could afford to put an extraordinary number of reporters on the street. Our journalism may be leaner in the future—and possibly less principled and idealistic.

Rick Rodriguez: Much confidence. It will take strong leadership, vision, the willingness to take risks and some failures, but we'll get there.

2. Looking specifically at print now. Do you think newspapers printed on paper are on a path to extinction? If not, what strategy is most likely to avoid extinction? (Investment, daring, urgency, calm, reinventing news delivery and audience or venturing into non-news online moneymakers?)

Phil Meyer: Extinction is unlikely. The successful local news product will probably be a hybrid with online providing most of the volume of content, and a smaller summary, perhaps less than daily, providing portability and the convenient scanning of print. The new magazine *The Week* is an interesting model.

Paul Ginocchio: Newspapers on paper may only be a 4-5 day a week event, with the other days online only. Printing facilities will be rationalized to third parties. Print subscriptions will rise in price so that the subscription revenue fully covers the paper, printing, distribution and administration surrounding the paper product—and most readers will get the product online. There will be a nominal online subscription fee and potentially, some papers will have a much higher fee if you want to get the news without advertising.

Rick Edmonds: I think the print newspaper is a survivor for at least 10 or 15 years—I hope to be alive and reading for at least that long and there are platoons of first wave baby boomers like me. Newspapers will keep having lots of cash to invest for some time to come. Proceeding "with all deliberate speed" makes sense and that is what newspapers seem to be doing. These big boats do not turn fast, but the industry needed to get a lot more urgent and has.

Rick Rodriguez: I think newspapers will be around for decades but will change. I think investigative journalism and other unique content are key to long-term survival. Newsrooms will have to run on multiple tracks—immediate postings through the web, daily paper, and paper and web longer term projects. I think other niche products that repackage the news and distribute it in various ways will continue to grow. So I don't believe we're on the path to extinction but on one that will require lots of change, including looking at ourselves as delivering news and information in lots of different ways.

Lou Ureneck: They are not headed to extinction, but certainly to contraction. I think that some people will always find newspapers on paper more convenient. But paper is expensive, so every square inch of it will be filled by only the highest and best uses, such as analytical journalism. Of course, stories will be shorter. Newsprint in the future will serve as the substrate for only the highest-end work or for readers who are wealthy enough, and willing, to pay for their preference for paper, I'm guessing. This trend will not be unlike the purpose that glossy paper now serves for some high-end magazines, such as the New Yorker. Routine content will find its way online. The migration of financial agate typifies what I think will become a growing trend.

John Carroll: Printed newspapers are declining, obviously. It's possible that the printed paper could become a luxury item, sold at a high price, which would save the medium. Or—another hope—it's possible that technology will preserve newspapers by allowing them to be printed out efficiently in the home, thus saving the costs of big presses, circulation departments, production departments, etc. Another technological fix: newspaper-like products that appear on tablet computers or on thin, lightweight computers that imitate the printed page. It's not print, but it could be quite similar…

3. Do you think the economic model of the Internet has to shift from an advertising based model to something else for traditional journalism to continue to thrive? If so, do you have any thoughts on what that new model might be?

Rick Rodriguez: I think print advertising is in many categories still more effective than online ads. That isn't necessarily true with classifieds, cars, travel and some others but many people just click through or block pop-ups and banners, even if they are creative. So the advertising model currently used isn't going to work. But does that mean people would be willing to shift and pay for content when basically they've received it for free with an internet connection. It will be difficult as well.

Rick Edmonds: That's unclear. Internet advertising has plenty of room to grow. Local search is at an infant stage and could be a goldmine. A mixture of free and paid premium content on the model of Times Select has potential too. The Bill Gates-Arthur Sulzberger presentation at ASNE persuaded me that Internet news will not look and read as it does now in another two or three years.

Paul Ginocchio: There will have to be some subscription revenues, but not as much as a print subscription. The print product will have to become a premium product to justify its cost and newspapers will outsource printing to third parties like Transcontinental (Canadian based printer). News gathering is only a small part of the total newspaper cost so it can survive on a pure ad model, as Phil Anschutz believes.

Lou Ureneck: Yes, I think future revenues will have to include higher proportion of fees from readers or users. As to a future model, this is the big question. We might be seeing the beginning of a return to some semblance, possibly, of private local ownership in places such as Philadelphia and St. Paul. Newspapers are profitable now and will be profitable in the future. The current crisis centers in large part on returns expected by investors who measure results against a range of businesses and whose only measure is financial. The financial problem in newspapers continues to be the gap between current stock-price expectations and predicted future streams of revenue. At some point, this gap is going to close, and it will close, I think, in the direction of permanently lower stock prices. That will settle some of the problem, though many people and institutions will have permanently loss significant stockholder "wealth." But it's a readjustment that tilts, I believe, in the direction of a healthier and more settled environment for journalism.

John Carroll: It would be good if newspapers and other providers of online content could (a) control the use of their content, and (b) charge for it. That would give them a greater degree of say in their own fates. With advertising rates set largely by others (Google, for example) and by extremely competitive markets, and with subscription revenue reduced nearly to zero, newspapers will be hard-pressed to sustain the large staffs that make them valuable. Giving our content away to all, even to our competitors, seems suicidal to me. Perhaps the resulting on-line ads will justify it, but I'm not yet convinced.

Phil Meyer: The "influence model" that I describe in *The Vanishing Newspaper* is certainly advertising based, and I think it could be applied to a community-based Internet publishing enterprise. We'll soon know because it's such an obvious strategy to try and the entry costs are low.

4. Now, looking at classified advertising, are papers doing everything they should to compete with Craigslist and others, including possibly, Google? If not, what should they be doing?

Phil Meyer: They should be trying more radical experiments and not leaving it to Newmark and Google to do all the innovating. But you can't blame newspapers for being conservative. It's a consequence of their easy-money history. It's why I think the important innovations will come from outside. There are more Craig Newmarks out there.

Lou Ureneck: Newspapers either need to manage the decline of classified as a revenue source until it finally becomes free, or find a way to add value to the newspaper classified. Craiglist has changed the business forever. With its sorting functions, it's as if the internet were designed for classifieds.

Paul Ginocchio: Newspapers are not promoting their websites enough and not aggressive enough in going out and getting new business—I believe they are still happy to wait for the classified customer to call them.

Rick Rodriguez: I'm not sure we should try to compete with Google, which has a worldwide audience. Our future is basically local and to that extent we should experiment to try to compete directly with craigslist. Are we doing enough as an industry? Obviously not.

John Carroll: The classified bonanza is over. It's going to be a tough, very competitive game from now on.

Rick Edmonds: Local search has enormous potential and newspapers are racing Google et al. to get there. No one has mixed the magic formula yet, though, and it's not clear (to me anyhow) whether newspapers or the big tech companies have the strategic advantage.

5. Circulation, revenue and newsroom investment data suggest that the newspapers most threatened right now are the big-city metro papers. How serious do you see this threat and what does it portend for state and local news? Would another news entity pick up that role or would citizens in end be left with little coverage of those institutions?

Paul Ginocchio: State and local news will still be covered, but not in the depth as it is today and it will have less prominence than in today's paper. Some of the coverage will be from citizens helping out.

Rick Edmonds: I don't yet see a case that blogs, citizen journalism and the like will emerge with a substitute for what big metros do best. However, like John Carroll, I am encouraged by recent indications that wealthy individuals, local group and/or not-for-profit entities will emerge, if necessary, to make sure communities have the degree of serious local news and public service they deserve.

Phil Meyer: More specialized media will pick up that role. The interesting problem will be defining their specialties. Much experimentation will take place, and the problem will be that not all of the experimenters will be journalists steeped in our public service tradition. The role of non-profits will become increasingly important as philanthropy takes on the watchdog task. An exciting, dangerous time lies ahead.

Lou Ureneck: It's a very serious situation, and I worry that the work of the big metros will not be picked up by smaller newspapers or local television stations.

John Carroll: I see no sign of other, smaller papers extending their reach to cover these larger stories. If the big metros disappeared, perhaps some would come forward.

6. What, if anything, will it take for newspapers to get more young people to become regular readers, either online or on paper?

Paul Ginocchio: Hire more young people and cover the news they care about, not just what the editors and journalists want to cover—even if it is soft news. Every newspaper should have an affiliated website to the main newspaper website which completely caters to the interests of 18-34 year olds with a completely different set of values on what news is important.

Rick Rodriguez: In our market [of Sacramento, CA], younger readers often pick up *The Bee*, just not often enough. I don't think younger readers are turned off to all newspapers. Some of them have told us in focus groups they like the paper, they just don't want to pay for it. Online has to be more dynamic and can't be a stagnant rehash of the day's paper with a few updates.

Rick Edmonds: Doom and gloom studies notwithstanding, I think a reasonable percentage of young adults are interested in news (and even newspapers) and that more will be as they age. Chasing those who are basically uninterested or non-readers has always seemed a fruitless exercise. Of course newspapers should be adaptive but they equally need some confidence in the importance and utility of what they do. Realistically, the audience may grow bolder, narrower, more educated and more elite. If so, so be it.

Phil Meyer: That would require a cultural change, but it's not impossible. If and when the international situation deteriorates to where we have to bring back the military draft, that alone might do it. More civics instruction in high schools, as David Mindich has suggested, would help. Whatever pulls young people's attention away from popular culture and points them toward the real world could help newspapers—and society.

John Carroll: There is no single fix. At a fundamental level, we need to cover basic news that young people want, such as high school sports. I'm skeptical that we can compete seriously with other, flashier, less ethical outfits that provide gossip and entertainment coverage. More dauntingly, we need to provide news in forms that are appealing to young people, which may require insights and skills we don't have at the moment.

7. If you could recommend one thing the newspaper industry would do differently what would that be?

John Carroll: The forty-year marriage of journalism and the modern corporation has failed. At the very time newspapers need enlightened stewardship, they are being actively harmed by their owners. Newspapers need a different form of ownership, one that values journalism, believes in public service and is unwilling — as a matter of principle and of long-term business strategy — to strangle newspapers for their short-term cash. Profit margins merely equal to the average among Fortune 500 companies would be a good start. That would allow newspapers to breathe again, to reverse their circulation losses, and to invest seriously in the online future.

Paul Ginocchio: Get a new ad salesforce, one that knows how to make cold calls and one that has no history of entitlement.

Lou Ureneck: Be bolder in their coverage of news. Seek truth over balance.

Rick Edmonds: Clarify to Wall Street that the news core must be kept strong, even at the expense of profit margins and earnings for a period of years because investments and experimentation in new media is essential too.

Phil Meyer: Transfer routine content to online, starting with the stock pages. Use the savings to invest in higher quality and more specialized content. Invest in radical experiments to find the right combination of newsprint and online distribution...

Local Journalism Is Flourishing

Damian Radcliffe

Damian Radcliffe is a journalism professor at Columbia University and regularly writes for ZDNet, a business technology news site.

F or the first time media is the least trusted institution globally," Edelman, the global PR and marketing firm concluded in its annual worldwide study on trust in institutions like the media, business and government.

These international findings are in line with recent data coming out of the U.S. A 2016 Gallup poll reported that just 32 percent of Americans trusted the mass media, while an Ipsos poll from summer 2018 found that nearly one-third of Americans agreed that the news media is the "enemy of the people."

How did it come to this?

First, it's important to recognize that our national media, just like our politics, has become highly partisan.

Second, it's necessary to acknowledge that existing media business models fuel this polarization. The drumbeat of an us-versus-them narrative has created what Tim Dixon, co-author of a new study titled "The Hidden Tribes of America," calls a "cartoonish view of the other side."

So what can be done to remedy this state of affairs?

Moving forward, I believe that local journalism—a key focus of my research and journalistic background—can play an important role in turning the tide and tackling this media malaise.

"How local journalism can upend the 'fake news' narrative," by Damian Radcliffe, The Conversation, November 30, 2018. https://theconversation.com/how-local-journalism-can-upend-the-fake-news-narrative-104630. Licensed under CC BY-ND 4.0.

The Trust Factor

Traditionally, the most important function of the Fourth Estate has been seen as watchdog reporting—journalism that holds authority to account.

But, this type of journalism is not exclusive to larger publications.

The impact and potential importance of these efforts at a local level can be seen each week in the "Local Matters" newsletter founded by the journalists Joey Cranney, Alexandra Glorioso and Brett Murphy.

It was also recognized last year when Art Cullen of The Storm Lake Times won the 2017 Pulitzer Prize in Editorial Writing. The twice-weekly newspaper in Iowa has nine-person staff and covers a town with a population of 10,000.

Yet Cullen beat fellow finalists from bigger papers—the Houston Chronicle and Washington Post - because he "successfully challenged powerful corporate agricultural interests in Iowa" in "editorials fueled by tenacious reporting, impressive expertise and engaging writing."

Research shows, however, that audiences don't just want local news outlets to be watchdogs. They want them to be a "good neighbor" too.

Local journalists are often the only journalists that most people will ever meet. So they play a significant role in how the wider profession is perceived.

For Caitlyn May, editor of the Cottage Grove Sentinel in Oregon, this means "it's essential that journalists leave the office and go out into the community." One way she does this is by holding a monthly, informal, "Meet the Editor" discussion at a local coffee shop.

Other outlets, such as the Dallas Morning News with their Curious Texas project, and KUOW Public Radio in Puget Sound, Washington, are partnering with a start-up called Hearken to encourage audiences to submit questions they want answered or suggest topics that they want local journalists to cover.

Poynter's 2018 Media Trust Survey identified that trust in local media is considerably higher than for national media. By blending watchdog reporting with community engagement, newsrooms can build on this foundation.

Local News on Shaky Ground

But what happens when local media disappears?

"Our sense of community and our trust in democracy at all levels suffer when journalism is lost or diminished," researchers at the University of North Carolina wrote in a recent report.

"In an age of fake news and divisive politics," they added, "the fate of communities across the country—and of grassroots democracy itself—is linked to the vitality of local journalism."

Indeed, data suggests a correlation between consumption of local news and civic engagement. This reinforces earlier research linking local media consumption and "institutionalized participation."

Put another way, if you consume local news, you're more likely to vote, contact local officials and participate in other forms of civic and democratic engagement.

Although many local newsrooms are going through a period of reinvention and reinvigoration, the sector needs to be on a more even financial keel if it is to successfully move forward. Outlets have to consistently produce high quality work in order to demonstrate their unique value to communities.

This isn't necessarily easy at a time when their are fewer journalists. Nearly half of all newsroom jobs—more than 20,000 of them—have disappeared in the past 20 years.

Recent research has highlighted the potential impact of these cuts at the local level.

Data produced by Duke University found that "less than half of the news provided by local media outlets is original. Only 17 percent is "truly local" in the sense that it's actually about events that have taken place within the city or town.

Journalism professor and researcher Jesse Holcomb has noted that local news outlets are still struggling to adapt to digital. He likens the internet to "an ill-fitting suit: functional, but not made for them."

Holcomb's analysis of 1,808 local news outlets revealed that less than half offer video content or newsletters. About one-in-10 local news outlets don't even have a website.

The Expanding News Deserts report, published in October by journalism professor Penny Muse Abernathy, showed that 171 U.S. counties do not have a local newspaper at all.

Nearly half all counties in the U.S.—1,449—have only one newspaper, and it's usually a weekly. Their research identified a net loss of almost 1,800 local newspapers since 2004.

Diminished resources—which may, in turn, lead to a less ambitious editorial mission—can have a profound impact on the health of our communities and democracy.

Looking Ahead

To succeed, local news providers must be relentlessly local and offer something different if they want people to pay for their product.

They also need to be more visible, embracing opportunities for real life engagement and consciously diversifying the range of people they interview.

According to a 2006 study by journalism professors Don Heider, Maxwell McCombs and Paula Poindexter, this means that investigative and watchdog reporting should appear alongside stories that demonstrate "caring about your community, highlighting interesting people and groups in the community, understanding the local community, and offering solutions to community problems."

That way, local journalists act as a check on those in power and create an informed citizenry, while also fostering a sense of community.

And local journalists don't just help communities make sense of the world around them. They're also a proxy for the wider news industry.

It's harder to believe that everything is "fake news" when the journalist you meet at back-to-school night, your kid's football practice, or in the local coffee shop is not just your neighbor, but someone who is also reporting on important local stories that you know to be true.

Journalism Is Broken, but Digital Journalism Can Fix It

Stuart Dredge

Stuart Dredge is an editor at Music Ally, a digital music industry news service. He also writes for the Guardian, *where he's contributing editor of their technology section.*

The growth of social media has changed the way news organisations cover conflicts around the world, but traditional journalistic values are still vital.

These, at least, were the main conclusions from a panel at the Web Summit conference in Dublin this morning, featuring representatives from Time, Vice News and News Corporation-owned social curation service Storyful.

"I'm not sure that the task of journalism has changed that much: we still send journalists to unearth stories and break news. But Twitter is our competition, and we have faced up to that reality," said Matt McAllester, Europe editor for Time.

"All legacy media organisations in the US and UK have gone through that process. And some have not survived."

While the panel shook their heads en masse when the phrase "citizen journalism" was mentioned, they admitted that on-the-spot witnesses are now as likely to be posting on social media as talking to a journalist.

"Twitter to us is a news source. Things break on Twitter," said Kevin Sutcliffe, head of news programming, EU at Vice News.

"Now people can bypass us using a camera phone and a social network, and the means of production have been completely overturned," added Mark Little, chief executive of Storyful. "Now everyone out there is a creator of content, and our job is more as managers of an overabundance of content."

The panel stressed that not all of the old values have been swept away. "It's really old-fashioned: can I find it out, is it true, can I stand by it? That level of trust is really important," said Sutcliffe. "I've got a story, but does it stand up, is it true, what are my sources?"

"There will be two types of parallel journalism going on—the facts on the ground from people who are there, foreign correspondents, and people like us who filter," said Little.

Some of the filters will be the same media organisations who employ on-the-ground correspondents, though. Time, for example, has a division focused on breaking news, which is deliberately kept separate from its foreign correspondents.

"We've hired a bunch of very young people in New York and Hong Kong and they're essentially aggregating as a breaking news service: when anything appears from a reliable news organisation, quickly write two or three paragraphs and get it out there," he said.

"That takes care of the news and it doesn't tax our correspondents. They do the premium you-can-only-get-it-here content that Vice News is [also] doing."

However, Little was more critical of the idea of news organisations covering breaking news. "Social media has proved to us that the breaking news model is broken for good. It's broken as a concept," he said.

"As a business, it's a really good business. But the concept that you, with the flashing 'breaking news' on the screen are going to be the first to break something is completely bullshit, because someone out there has witnessed it."

He described Storyful's approach, which focuses on finding those witnesses' online posts, and bringing them to a wider audience. "The key thing for us is to find the first piece of content that will define a story: the video, the tweet… we have 40 journalists looking in real-time for the original source," he said.

"For us the most important thing is who's the person on the ground with the camera-phone standing there right now. Authenticity has replaced authority as the new currency of this environment."

Authenticity is sometimes a false currency, however: photographs claiming to show a bombing in one country may have been taken in another several months before, while false Twitter rumours can spread rapidly in the wake of a natural disaster or terrorist attack.

Little suggested that there's increasingly a self-policing aspect to social media. "There's never been a better way to spread a hoax than social media, but there's never been a better fact-checking desk than social media," he said.

In an earlier session, Anne-Marie Tomchak, presenter and producer at BBC Trending, made a similar claim. "It's not just journalists who are asking lots of questions about what's being shared online," she said. "Social media users have become really discerning about what they're seeing."

In the later session, the trio of journalists were optimistic about the appetite for hard news and foreign affairs among the "millennials" who are the most active demographic on social media, with Sutcliffe reiterating a claim that Vice executives have made regularly in recent months.

"It's come out of a really interesting debate in heritage news, that young people were not interested in news, and they were not going to watch anything longer than two minutes online, probably featuring a cat," he said.

"What we've found over the last six months, we've overturned the sense that there isn't an interest from this age group for news, current affairs and the world. It's enormous and it's growing exponentially."

McAllester suggested that 5-10 years ago "the orthodoxy was the world doesn't care about foreign news" and agreed that modern, online outlets have put paid to the idea. "What Vice, BuzzFeed, Mashable and numerous startups are doing by hiring [foreign] correspondents and getting amazing traffic," he said.

That's incredibly encouraging to even an old brand like Time," he said. "We all need competition. I absolutely see the BuzzFeed correspondent in the Middle East as competition… and that's very encouraging."

Sutcliffe suggested that the 24-hour television news cycle has become "slightly worn out", suggesting that the news agenda in that world is driven by "everybody running in one direction after one story" rather than digging for new stories.

"What we're commissioning is what we think is interesting and you should know about, and that can be anywhere," he said. "We'll do Ukraine and the big stories… but over there, that place that nobody's bothering to go, that's important too. We're not chasing after other media organisations and their agenda."

In her presentation, Tomchak praised the response of Twitter users to persecution and killings by the Islamic State organisation.

She cited the #WeAreN campaign, where people changed their avatars to a sign painted by ISIS members on Christians' houses marking them out, in solidarity with those people, as well as the movement to share an image of executed journalist James Foley when he was alive, to crowd out images shared by Islamic State supporters of his beheading.

Tomchak also suggested that while Twitter tends to be the focus for these kinds of campaigns, as well as breaking news, mobile messaging apps like WhatsApp and FireChat have an important role to play.

"I truly believe that chat apps are and will increasingly become the place in which we will distribute our news, and the place in which we find stories, and the place in which we gather news," she said. "Social media is a place for political, cultural and social change… and it is also one of the newest weapons in war," she said.

In his session, Storyful's Little warned that journalists must not underestimate the attempts by governments to subvert this role for social media.

"New forms of journalism will emerge. We're in an arms race now from the NSA to the Chinese government, tying to close down freedom of expression, and use social media against itself," he said. "We are on the opposite side."

Convenience and Accessibility Provide Net Benefits

Katerina Eva Matsa and Elisa Shearer

Katerina Eva Matsa is an associate director at the Pew Research Center. Elisa Shearer is a research associate at the Pew Research Center.

About two-thirds of American adults (68%) say they at least occasionally get news on social media, about the same share as at this time in 2017, according to a new Pew Research Center survey. Many of these consumers, however, are skeptical of the information they see there: A majority (57%) say they expect the news they see on social media to be largely inaccurate. Still, most social media news consumers say getting news this way has made little difference in their understanding of current events, and more say it has helped than confused them (36% compared with 15%).

Republicans are more negative about the news they see on social media than Democrats. Among Republican social media news consumers, 72% say they expect the news they see there to be inaccurate, compared with 46% of Democrats and 52% of independents. And while 42% of those Democrats who get news on social media say it has helped their understanding of current events, fewer Republicans (24%) say the same.[1] Even among those Americans who say they *prefer* to get news on social media over other platforms (such as print, TV or radio), a substantial portion (42%) express this skepticism.

Asked what they like about the news experience on social media, more Americans mention ease of use than content. "Convenience" is by far the most commonly mentioned benefit, (21%), while 8% say they most enjoy the interactions with other

"News Use Across Social Media Platforms 2018," by Katerina Eva Matsa and Elisa Shearer, Pew Research Center, Washington, DC (September 10, 2018). https://www.journalism. org/2018/09/10/news-use-across-social-media-platforms-2018/. Used in accordance with Pew Research Center reuse Policy. http://www.pewresearch.org/terms-and-conditions/. Usage in no way implies endorsement.

people. Fewer social media news consumers say they most like the diversity of the sources available (3%), or the ability to tailor the content they see (2%).

This study is based on a survey conducted July 30-Aug. 12, 2018, among 4,581 U.S. adults who are members of Pew Research Center's nationally representative American Trends Panel.

Growth in Social Media News Consumption Slows Down

About two-thirds of U.S. adults (68%) get news on social media sites, about the same as the portion that did so in 2017 (67%). One-in-five get news there often.

Facebook is still far and away the site Americans most commonly use for news, with little change since 2017. About four-in-ten Americans (43%) get news on Facebook. The next most commonly used site for news is YouTube, with 21% getting news there, followed by Twitter at 12%. Smaller portions of Americans (8% or fewer) get news from other social networks like Instagram, LinkedIn or Snapchat.

The prominence of each social media site in the news ecosystem depends on two factors: its overall popularity and the extent to which people see news on the site.

Reddit, Twitter and Facebook stand out as the sites where the highest portion of users are exposed to news – 67% of Facebook's users get news there, as do 71% of Twitter's users and 73% of Reddit users. However, because Facebook's overall user base is much larger than those of Twitter or Reddit, far more Americans overall get news on Facebook than on the other two sites.

The other sites studied—including YouTube,Tumblr, Instagram, LinkedIn, Snapchat and WhatsApp—have less of a news focus among their user base. Fewer than half of each site's users get news on each platform. Still both YouTube and LinkedIn saw these portions rise over the past year.

Nearly four-in-ten YouTube users (38%) say they get news on YouTube, slightly higher than the 32% of users who did so last year. And 30% of LinkedIn users get news there, up from 23% in 2017.

The percentage of U.S. adults who get news on two or more social media sites is 28%, little changed from 2017 (26%).

Demographics of Social Media News Consumers

Social media sites' news consumers can look vastly different in terms of their demographic makeup. For example, the majority of news consumers on Instagram are nonwhite. Three-quarters of Snapchat's news consumers are ages 18 to 29, more than any other site. And LinkedIn, Twitter and Reddit's news consumers are more likely to have bachelor's degrees—61% of LinkedIn's news consumers do, as do 46% of Reddit's news consumers and 41% of Twitter's news consumers.

Most Social Media News Consumers Are Concerned About Inaccuracy, but Many Still See Benefits

Even though a substantial portion of U.S. adults at least occasionally get news on social media, over half (57%) of these news consumers say they *expect* the news they see on social media to be largely inaccurate. This is consistent with the low trust in news from social media seen in past surveys. About four-in-ten (42%) expect the news they see on social media to be largely accurate.

Republicans are more likely than Democrats and independents to be concerned with the inaccuracy of the news they see on social media. Among social media news consumers, about three-quarters of Republicans say this (72%), compared with 46% of Democrats and about half of independents (52%). And, while there are some age differences in expectations of the accuracy of social media news, this party divide persists regardless of age.

Concerns about the inaccuracies in news on social media are prevalent even among those who say they *prefer* to get their news there—among this group, 42% say that they expect the news they see to largely be inaccurate. Still, those social media news consumers who prefer other platforms such as print or television for news are even more likely to say they expect the news on social media to be largely inaccurate.

Not only do social media news consumers expect the news they see there to be inaccurate, but inaccuracy is the *top* concern they bring up about information on social media. When asked an open-ended question about what they dislike most about getting news on social media, concerns about inaccuracy top the list, outstripping concerns about political bias and the bad behavior of others.[2] Specifically, about three-in-ten (31%) social media news consumers say that inaccuracy is what they dislike most about the experience. Included in the responses about inaccuracy were concerns about unreliable sources, lack of fact checking, and "fake news."

Politics surface as another negative aspect of social media, though at a lower rate—11% who at least occasionally get news there say there is too much bias or political opinion, either on the part of the news organizations or the people on the platform. About the same share of social media news consumers (10%) say they dislike the low quality of news—such as lack of in-depth coverage, or clickbait-style headlines.

Convenience and Ease Seen As Most Enjoyable Part of Getting News on Social Media

Even though social media news consumers have concerns about the accuracy of the information there, they also cite some benefits of getting news on social media, which may help explain why getting news on the platform is still so common.

The most commonly named positive thing about getting news on social media is convenience—21% say this is what they liked most, with responses such as "It's very accessible," "It's available at the touch of a button" and "I don't have to go looking for it."

Respondents also say they like the interpersonal element: 8% of social media news consumers say they enjoy interacting with others— whether through discussing the news, sharing news with friends and family, or seeing what others' opinions are. Speed and timeliness are also mentioned as positive aspects of getting news on social media—7% say they like how quick it is to get news on social media, and 6% say they like that news there is up to date, with descriptions like "up to the minute" or "the most current."

A fair share of respondents (12%) say they do not like *anything* about getting news on social media. This is higher than the percentage who volunteered that they do not *dislike* anything about news on social media in the previous question (only 4% say this).

About a Third Say Social Media Positively Affects Their Understanding of Current Events

About a third (36%) of the people who get news on social media say it has helped them better understand current events. Nearly half (48%) say it doesn't have much of an effect on their understanding, and 15% say that news on social media has made them *more* confused about current events.

Among those who get news on social media, Republicans are less positive than Democrats and independents about how news there influences their understanding of the world around them: About a quarter (24%) say that social media news helps them better understand current events, compared with 42% of Democrats and 40% of independents.

Age is also a factor in the way people view the role of social media. Younger social media news consumers are more likely to say it has impacted their learning for the better. About half of social media news consumers ages 18 to 29 (48%) say news on social media makes them better informed, compared with 37% of those 30 to 49, 28% of those 50 to 64, and 27% of those 65 and older.

Notes

1 The difference by party support remains even when accounting for the fact that Republicans are less likely to prefer social media as a platform for news.

2 Respondents were asked to list the things they like and dislike most about news on social media before being asked if they expected the news there to be accurate or inaccurate.

A Wider Reach Isn't Always Better

Ying Chan

Ying Chan is a founding director of the University of Hong Kong's Journalism and Media Studies Centre. Chan also teaches at Columbia University's Graduate School of Journalism and has written for the Nation *and the* Village Voice *and has reported for* 60 Minutes *and* Dateline.

D igitization is one of the primary driving forces behind recent changes in journalism, including news values, professional ethics, workflows, working conditions, and newsroom management. The Mapping Digital Media study shows that digital media have not only changed journalism practices in developed countries but have also significantly shaped the way journalists work in emerging markets. Digital media bring opportunities, risks, and challenges to journalism. While digitization facilitates news gathering and dissemination, it does not necessarily foster better journalism. Plagiarism, lack of verification, and other unethical journalistic practices have increased alarmingly in many countries.

Specifically, when it comes to investigative journalism, digitization has created new publishing platforms and dissemination channels for professional journalists and aspiring citizen reporters alike, but in the majority of countries investigative reports do not seem to be having an increased social impact. Some MDM country reports claim that digitization has wrought havoc on investigative journalism.

While digitization provides opportunities for citizen journalists and independent media to conduct their own research and investigation and in turn publish and distribute their reports, in

"Journalism and Digital Times: Wider Reach and Sloppy Reporting," by Ying Chan, Open Society Foundations, https://www.opensocietyfoundations.org/uploads/02fc2de9-f4a5-4c07-8131-4fe033398336/mapping-digital-media-overviews-20140828.pdf, September 16, 2014. Reprinted by permission.

many countries the accountability of such original content created by citizen journalists is questionable.

The emergence of digital media has enabled minority groups to have a voice in the public arena, but it has not shifted the traditional media's practice of covering sensitive issues in a restricted, biased, or sensational manner.

Almost all candidates in general elections use social media platforms to communicate with voters, but the emergence of new political actors *because* of digitization is something that has occurred in only a few countries. Digital media have, however, remarkably increased the volume of political discussion and raised the political interest of the general public.

Risks and Opportunities for Good-Quality Journalism

Digitization brings new opportunities to journalists in three notable respects: faster news delivery, better access to sources and information, and more interaction with readers. Nearly two-thirds of the 56 countries in the study noted that digitization had quickened news production and delivery cycles, trends that are most remarkable in countries in Asia and in North and South America. In about half of the countries, most of which are emerging economies such as China, Brazil, India, and South Africa, digital media have provided more sources and information to journalists. In almost all the countries digital media enhanced the interaction between the editorial team and readers, making it easier for reporters to learn about customers' reading habits and interests.

In Germany, for example, digital technology has not only given journalists the possibility of reaching more sources but it also has let them dig into the details of a story to improve their copy. In Canada, meanwhile, digitization has enabled the creation of large databases and archives that allow journalists to retrieve background information much faster than was the case in the analog world. Building stronger relationships with readers and viewers has been one of the biggest benefits that digitization has brought to journalists:

> Digital transformations in the newsroom and in use out in the field have enabled journalists to exploit digital media tools to their advantage. By enhancing their ability to retrieve information through search engines and smartphones, locating sources and building relationships with new and old audiences through j-blogs and social networking sites and democratizing the former role of the copy taster, journalists are able to widen their source base and improve their interview questions when under pressure.

Similar trends are found in Singapore where "the internet has become an important source for news stories, a crucial platform for distributing news, as well as receiving instant feedback from readers."

However, digitization has also posed challenges and risks to journalistic standards as the news cycle shrinks, and the internet has made it more convenient for journalists to commit plagiarism. In more than half the countries, reporters pay less attention to verifying the facts and sources for their stories. The prevalent use of published materials and rumors in news stories has posed "the most pervasive threats" that digitization has brought to journalism.

In developed countries such as the United States, the United Kingdom, and Finland, as well as developing countries like China, South Africa, Brazil, India, and Egypt, there were declines in original content and increasing copy-and-paste journalism in the news media. An equal number of emerging and developed economies reports noted practices like prevalent plagiarism, violation of copyright law, or quoting without attribution. Such practices span a broad spectrum of countries, ranging from the United States and Canada in North America, and Egypt, Kenya and South Africa in Africa, to Asian countries like China, Japan, India, and Indonesia.

Time pressures and fast-paced journalism have made journalists more prone to mistakes. In Brazil, "the quality of news has been compromised by an editorial workflow that privileges speed over accuracy. The race to deliver news as fast as possible can lead to deficient revision practices and inconsistent fact checking, along with a tendency to reproduce content as it is received—in the format of, for example, press releases—as opposed to properly finding and checking sources."

In Malaysia, newspaper editors said that plagiarism was very easy online using the copy-and-paste function. According to Yong Soo Heong, editor-in-chief of Bernama, Malaysia's state-owned news agency: "Previously, some news editors would say 'Do not read the Bernama ticker tape,' and come up with an original story first. But we can't do that now because everyone can read online and search Wikipedia or Google."

Digitization has also posed a threat in terms of data security and individual privacy. In almost a fifth of the countries, digitization has made the theft of information and the illegal interception of conversations easier. Countries experiencing this include largely Eurasian countries such as Russia, China, and India, and those African countries where there is greater connectivity, such as Kenya and Morocco. In the United States, potential leaks of information pose a bigger threat to good journalism than plagiarism. The United States report cited the State Department cables released by WikiLeaks and observed that "it is clear that the possibilities of involuntary institutional transparency are considerable, and this has forced the journalism profession in the United States to examine how to engage with sources that hold massive caches of data."

The working conditions for journalists have generally worsened as a result of digitization. As news production has become faster with higher information volumes being generated, journalists are increasingly expected to work longer hours and possess diverse digital skills. Journalists in the digital age not only write articles but also shoot and edit images and videos, and manage social media, all of which increases their workload. In the context of tightening financial resources and increasing competition, journalists' working conditions have been deteriorating as they are required to work extra hours and assume new roles to accommodate demands that derive from digital news delivery.

Perhaps the biggest role that digitalization plays in journalism lies in news gathering and dissemination rather than in news quality. In France,

> The expansion of online news has not substantially enlarged the volume of valuable information, as most content is still based on the same sources as before digitization: press agencies, press conferences, or internal sources of information. It is rather a system of dissemination of the news (the hypermedia system) that has changed, as similar content is now delivered on the main websites, commented on by blogs, and promoted on Twitter and Facebook.

Digitization has become a watershed for good and average journalism. One journalist, Bernard Poulet, said that "digitization has the same effects on journalism that globalization has on the middle class," comparing digitization with the death of the middle class of journalists. Mr Poulet projected that the profession of journalism will split into two distinct groups: a majority of "blue-collar" underpaid journalists, performing routine tasks and "feeding the machine," and a few high-ranking journalists with great expertise and a unique personal style, whose names might even become brands.

Digital media are likely to trigger changes in media structure in countries where news remains heavily censored. In China, in the last few years

> many media have been transformed from tools for party propaganda into semi-autonomous, market-oriented media. During this change, the party line has weakened while market influences have been strengthened, solemn news reporting has decreased while human interest stories, entertainment news, and tabloid journalism have abruptly increased. These changes have profoundly influenced the public's news demands, the media's news offer, and the role of journalists.

Watchdog Journalism

Digital media have created unprecedented opportunities for investigative journalists, with new publishing platforms and distribution channels. More than 60 percent of the countries have seen a surge in new publishing platforms such as blogs, independent websites, and email groups for investigative journalism. The encouraging trends span the spectrum of countries from emerging economies such as China, India, Kenya, Egypt, Morocco, and Brazil to developed economies such as the United States and France.

However, less than one-third of the countries noted that digital media have helped to expand the social impact of investigative reports. In Asian countries such as China, India, Pakistan, Malaysia, and Thailand, digitization facilitated the production and dissemination of investigative reports and helped them enlarge their social impact. In some European countries, such as Russia and Germany, the impact of investigative journalism in the digital age has been increasing due to digital platforms. In contrast, in several Latin American and Western European countries, the impact of investigative reports on the digital side was limited. These countries include the Netherlands and Spain, and Mexico, Peru, and Argentina.

In India, there are several digital media platforms that publish investigative reports, such as Indiareport.com, Youthcurry. blogspot.com, and Churumuri.wordpress.com. The impact of the investigative reports published on these platforms is amplified by television news channels and social media networks and has resulted in the resignation or arrest of senior government officials and high-profile politicians and corporate executives.

In Pakistan, the proliferation of media outlets has helped to increase the audiences and reach of investigative stories. Thanks also to cross-media ownership, media groups have been able to promote their investigative work across platforms. At the same time, the internet has become the main publication alternative for content that is not published or broadcast by mainstream media outlets owing to pressure from the state, advertisers, and political parties. The reach of these stories is further amplified by social media such as Twitter and Facebook that are widely used by media groups to promote news content. Other online platforms such as YouTube give journalistic content a longer shelf life. Investigative journalism has had a social impact in Pakistan, even though there is a blurring line between leaks, whistleblowing, and real investigative reporting:

> Anonymous contributions featuring violent incidents or documenting abuses of power via internet have led to judicial inquiries and prosecutions. In particular, the blog of Malala has drawn the world's attention to the threat posed by militancy to girls' education. The attack she survived from Taliban militants led to national and international condemnation and has sparked a global activist movement on behalf of girls' education.

In Jordan, there has been a "big response by society and the government to investigative journalists' video evidence." An investigative piece by the Arab Reporters for Investigative Journalism (ARIJ)[1] was picked up by local news websites and subsequently tweeted, re-tweeted, and posted on Facebook. This triggered a flood of intense commentary and helped spark a public debate, which in the end inspired competitors to run their own investigations. For example, the investigation of abuses at private centers for the handicapped spurred public outrage, prompting the king himself to visit the centers and demand punishment for those responsible.

Similar trends are found in Japan where the "internet is a useful information source and study tool for investigative journalists." In Armenia, as well, where investigative reporting has traditionally been rare, digitization has multiplied the readers of investigative reports. In Argentina, mobile phones have played a remarkable role in disseminating investigative reports: "Digitization, including mobile phones, cameras and the internet, has saved the cost of journalist enquiry." The positive impact on investigative journalism is also noted in Brazil where "digitization improved the dissemination and effectiveness of investigative reports."

Even in China, where the government imposes tight control on news media and journalists, investigative reporting is being revamped in the age of the internet:

> Social media have become a vanguard for breaking censorship and creating space for traditional media to report stories they could not years ago. More importantly, they are making investigative reporting into a process rather than a product. Twitter-like microblogging as well as conventional blogging have added further possibilities that allow journalists not only to publish what has been investigated, but to turn the investigation into a public conversation and ask for tips.

A particular phenomenon in China is microblogging and its massive impact on journalism: "It breaks the boundaries of news organizations, and investigative reporters, even if they are competitors, tend to form a temporary community on microblogs for information-gathering to meet their various needs ... The image of the investigative reporter as a lone wolf is no longer correct."

Digitization has made possible big data and data journalism, which is another approach to promoting government transparency and accountability. In almost all the MDM countries, the internet makes it easier for journalists today to access and compare data. Increasingly digital platforms have been boosting data-driven journalism. Digitization was very often mentioned by journalists interviewed for this project as a driving force behind the creation and use of databases. Data-driven journalism has been developing fast in Western Europe and North America, with Eastern Europe coming up fast behind.

For investigative journalism, the biggest, most unequivocal gain from digitization by far has been the extended access to sources, information, and data. is has happened in approximately 80 percent of the countries in the project.

Meanwhile, digital media have posed new challenges for investigative journalism. The most common problems include hacking websites; reporters and sources being followed, monitored, and threatened; prosecution; the theft of information; difficulties in reaching sources; and the interception of information by the government.

In addition, the fast and huge flow of news has adversely affected investigative journalism. In countries as varied as Japan, Russia, Slovakia, Estonia, and India multiple forms of digital media, increasing numbers of media outlets, fierce media competition, and journalists' pressure to break news have led to the inclusion of erroneous, misleading, and misinterpreted information in the news. There is unverified or biased coverage even in investigative reports. In Malaysia, journalists' exaggerated reliance on user-generated content such as Wikipedia led to misreporting. In Moldova there have also been more misleading and misinterpreted data in journalistic stories.

In Canada, although the ways in which digitization has improved or hindered investigative journalism are still unclear, new opportunities are being made available through digital media tools for sources to contact journalists and for journalists to discover new sources. The digitization of huge volumes of information has improved access, particularly access to government documents. Yet digitization has also increased the demand for immediacy in news delivery: the drive to be there, live, on location. Investigative journalism suffers in this context as the news content suffers in quality. The negative impact of time pressure on journalists' output has been also noted in India:

> The frenetic pace, partially set by digitization and partly by competition, has led to mistakes, even blunders. In addition, round- the-clock schedules leave reporters and editors with less time to pursue serious, long-term, in-depth investigations. Apart from a few print publications, mainstream television channels and websites have been unable to pursue investigative journalism seriously. Even though access to information has become easier, few journalists have been trained or take the time to wade through the enormous amount of data available online.

A phenomenon that has not been spawned by digitization and that survives in many countries, badly affecting the editorial output and the journalistic profession, is self-censorship. Countries as varied as Nigeria, Nicaragua, Guatemala, and China have continued to experience the bad effects of self-censorship on investigative reporting in particular. In China above all, there have been numerous threats to investigative journalism:

> In the digital age, investigative journalism still encountered obstacles from the government, social organizations, and individuals, in the form of state supervision systems and the self-censorship practices of both media and individuals. Professional journalists who publish sensitive stories still face punishment such as loss of status, reduced wages, being fired, or permanent expulsion from the media community. Also, the government has not allowed websites to be set up to host investigations into specialized subjects or themes, such as corruption, human rights, energy and the environment, health and safety.

In Japan, "investigative reporting by mainstream mass media still has the most influence and gains the most public attention." Although there has also been some investigative reporting by independent and eminent individuals, most of them "have reached an advanced age and rarely publish on the internet."

The findings of the MDM reports are supported by leading journalists and experts. Dick Tofel, president of the American-based nonprofit news organization ProPublica, says that big data along with new ways to tell stories are two key trends shaping the future of investigative journalism. "Investigative journalists can cover new and different kinds of stories using big data sets and digital storytelling. Using data to let people localize national stories is just one important way that investigative journalism is changing for the better."[2]

Aron Phihofer, associate managing editor of digital strategy at *The New York Times*, and Francesca Panetta, audio producer at *The Guardian*, have also noted that "digital doesn't mean the death of investigative and long form journalism," citing award-winning projects such as "Snow Fall" and "Firestorm."[3] Barry Sussman, editor of the Nieman Watchdog Project, agrees that websites have created new multimedia platforms for news organizations to display their investigative pieces. Nonprofit entities and individuals are also given the chance to publish their own investigative work. However, few investigative assignments will be or should be completed online. It is still important to work with actual sources. "Databases, and the computer tools we have to work with, are a terrific resource," he said, "but there still need to be stories about real people and real people's lives."[4]

[…]

Notes

1. The Amman-based Arab Reporters for Investigative Journalism was formed in early 2005 to support independent high-quality professional journalism.

2. Susan Gunelius, "The Future is Bright for Non-Profit Investigative Journalism," at http://newstex.com/2014/ 01/15/the-future-is-bright-for-non-profit-investigative-journalism.

3. "Investigative Journalism: the Future's Digital," at http://www.tcij.org/resources/investigative-journalism-futures- digital.

4. Barry Sussman, "Digital Journalism: Will It Work for Investigative Journalism?," at http://www.nieman.harvard. edu/reports/article/100073/Digital-Journalism-Will-It-Work-for-Investigative-Journalism.aspx.

Local Journalism Is in Decline

Andrea Macko

Andrea Macko was a journalist and columnist for the St. Marys Journal Argus *in Canada until the newspaper was shuttered in 2017.*

There's a perception that small towns never change. But my small town—bucolic St. Marys, Ont.—can now mark the passage of time from one specific day, almost a year ago: Nov. 27, 2017.

That day, the St. Marys Journal Argus and more than 20 other community weekly newspapers were suddenly shuttered by Postmedia Network Canada Corp. The papers were purchased from Torstar Corp., and immediately closed in an apparent effort to strengthen community newspapers by eliminating competition.

To say that "the Journal" was as much of St. Marys as our namesake cement concern or scenic trestle walkway is a gross understatement. For starters, our community newspaper actually predated the town it served. The St. Marys Journal began publishing in 1853, a year before the incorporation of the village (now town) of St. Marys. The Argus first went to press in 1857. The two papers merged almost a century ago.

By the time my husband and I moved from Toronto to St. Marys in 2003, the Journal was the archetypical small-town paper, earnestly reporting on all facets of small-town life, from municipal politics to school plays to giant produce. There was no other way to learn about our new hometown or to meet the characters who made it tick.

I learned all the more when I joined the Journal as a full-time reporter in 2005. The job tested my professional mettle in ways my former life as a fashion editor never could. The weekly hamster wheel of community reportage is not for the faint of mind or body.

"My small-town newspaper died a year ago. The community has been grieving ever since," by Andrea Macko, The Globe and Mail (Toronto), November 26, 2018. Reprinted by permission.

I would eventually travel down a different career path, but I came to contribute a weekly column to the Journal—when the lifestyle/recipe columnist retired after an incredible 60 years, I jumped at the chance to return to the lighter side of news.

I also kept my feet professionally wet by covering vacation leaves. When I joined the Journal, there were three in the news department. By 2017, there was nobody in the news department other than the indefatigable Stew Slater, who wrote for the Journal as a high-school student and returned full-time when I departed to begin my family. (The sports department was solely in the hands of Pat Payton, a 30-year veteran of the position.)

I had covered for Stew the week prior to Nov. 27. When I came into the office that Monday morning, Stew's tone was unforgettably taut as he cut short my conversation. "The Journal's done. It doesn't matter any more."

In the news release announcing the closure, which also affected a supplementary publication called the Weekender, Postmedia spelled "St. Marys" wrong. Had the Journal ever inserted a possessive apostrophe into our town's name, a crowd of indignant readers would have stormed the office. For a national media company to make the mistake was strongly symbolic.

One hundred and sixty-four years of informing civic life, ripped from my community on a sunny Monday morning.

A year on, I still can't believe that my hand was the last to ever shape the Journal. I regret that we couldn't cover our biggest news story—Postmedia's fatal low blow was made all the lower because it immediately halted operations at its newly acquired papers. We couldn't analyze our demise or say thank you and farewell to our readers.

I tearfully posted my reaction to Facebook the night of the closure. A few days later, our municipality graciously released a statement from Stew. Comforts—but cold comforts when your life's work was delivered weekly on newsprint.

St. Marys still benefits from a weekly, independently owned newspaper. As competitors do, it has a different feel than the Journal did. With a youthful history and a renegade spirit, the St. Marys Independent continues to evolve as the sole voice of our town.

It's easy to dismiss the need for good journalism in smaller communities. The stories may not seem as sexy as Donald Trump's latest dust-up or some new environmental disaster, but these microcosms—what small town hasn't had an outspoken mayor or a suspicious smell emanating from a pillar of industry?—have a much greater effect on daily lives.

The responsible spread of information and analysis is not as simple as starting a blog, or sharing on social media. Many St. Marys residents don't use social media for a variety of reasons, from lack of access, to age, to a desire for privacy in a place where everyone already knows you. As a result, platforms such as Facebook community pages only reach a portion of our population. Digital saturation remains years away, if it ever occurs at all.

For many, the physical act of picking up a paper remains the easiest way to be informed. Admittedly, journalism is fraught with challenges, especially in a small town where lives and interests are often entwined in complex ways. But small-town journalists can't hide behind a byline: When you face your audience at every turn of the day, you must work in a way that allows you to always hold your head high.

A few months after the Journal's closure, St. Marys's community museum mounted an exhibition-cum-tribute on local newspapers. Amid the clippings of notable stories—threats of hospital closure, a visit from Terry Fox and debates over municipal debentures—one of the informative panels noted that after being family-owned for almost 150 years, the Journal was sold in 1999 to the Metroland chain (a Torstar subsidiary). It was a time when globalism, and the internet's potential, were gleaming with promise.

"The paper continued to publish under the new owners but now it was only a small cipher in the cut-throat world of national media," the panel aptly stated. How sacred is one newspaper when an entire chain of print and digital communities must be considered in the bottom line?

Corporate ownership was a slow vise on the Journal and its ilk. By Nov. 27, 2017, it didn't take much effort to close the clamps.

After the Journal's demise, visitors to its homepage were redirected to one of two "local" Postmedia papers, which, at 20 and 30 minutes down the road, might as well be a different universe for St. Marysites. I suspect other communities that lost their papers feel the same.

It's a different universe for the families whose generations of birth, marriage and death notices would all have appeared in the Journal. It's certainly a different universe for those who anticipated "Journal Wednesday," and the visit to our community post office for their copy and subsequent chat with acquaintances while there.

It's definitely a different universe for all the stories that now go untold in communities lacking a news outlet. Fundraisers that aren't successful due to lack of publicity. Political decisions that go unquestioned because there's no reporter to ask. Lives less informed and engaged.

When stories, good or bad, are no longer shared, it's all the easier to believe that nothing changes in a small town. Apathy grows, and communities wither as a result.

Earlier this week, as the first anniversary of the death of the Journal approached, the federal government pledged almost $600-million in funding to Canada's news industry. Hopefully, it will help another small town avoid the same fate as St. Marys. For the Journal Argus, it came too late.

Digital Media Is a Slippery Slope

Margaret Simons

Margaret Simons was director of the Centre for Advancing Journalism at the University of Melbourne in Australia. She is currently an associate professor of journalism at Monash University, Australia.

Australia's two largest legacy media organisations recently announced big cuts to their journalistic staff. Many editorial positions, perhaps up to 120, will disappear at Fairfax Media, publisher of The Age and The Sydney Morning Herald, and News Corporation announced the sacking of most of its photographers and editorial production staff.

Both announcements were accompanied by corporate spin voicing a continuing commitment to quality journalism. Nobody in the know believes it. This is the latest local lurch in a crisis that is engulfing journalism worldwide.

Now, partly thanks to Donald Trump, many more people are turning their mind to the future of news, including "fake" news and its opposite.

How, in the future, are we to know the difference between truth, myth and lies?

Almost too late, there is a new concern for the virtues of the traditional newsroom, and what good journalists do. That is, find things out, verify the facts and publish them in outlets which, despite famous stuff-ups, can generally be relied upon to provide the best available version of the truth.

As this week's announcements make clear, the newsrooms that have traditionally provided most original journalism are radically shrinking.

"Journalism faces a crisis worldwide – we might be entering a new dark age," by Margaret Simons, Guardian News and Media Limited, April 15, 2017. Reprinted by permission.

News media for most of the last century appeared to be one relatively simple business. Gather an audience by providing content, including news. Sell the attention of the audience to advertisers.

The internet and its applications have brought that business undone. As any householder can attest, the audience no longer assembles in the same concentrations. The family no longer gathers around the news on television. Most homes have multiple screens and news is absorbed as it happens.

"Appointment television" is nearly dead, at least for those under 50.

At the same time, technology has torn apart the two businesses — advertising and news—that used to be bound together by the physical artefact of the newspaper. Once, those who wanted to find a house, a job or a car had to buy a newspaper to read the classifieds. Now, it is cheaper and more efficient to advertise and search online, without needing to pay a single journalist.

Publishers and broadcasters have moved online, but the advertising model fails. Ads on websites earn a fraction of the amount that used to be charged for the equivalent in a newspaper or during a program break.

All this is last century's news—but over the past five years the landscape has shifted again because of the dominance of Google (which also owns YouTube) and Facebook. These social media engines have quickly become the world's most powerful publishers. Besides them, Murdoch looks puny. Yet Google and Facebook don't employ journalists. They serve advertisements and news to the audience members on the basis of what they know about their interests.

For advertisers, it's all gravy. Why pay for a display ad in a newspaper when you can have your material delivered direct to the social media feeds of people who you know are likely to be interested in buying your product?

It is now estimated that of every dollar spent on advertising in the western world, 90 cents ends up in the pockets of Google and Facebook.

Today, just about anyone with an internet connection and a social media account has the capacity to publish news and views to the world. This is new in human history.

The last great innovation in communications technology, the printing press, helped bring about the enlightenment of the 1500s and 1600s.

The optimists among us thought the worldwide web and its applications might lead to a new enlightenment—but as has become increasingly clear, the reverse is also possible. We might be entering a new dark age.

Fake news isn't new. The place of Barack Obama's birth was about as verifiable as a fact gets—with the primary document, his birth certificate, published online. But the mere publication of a fact did not stop a large proportion of US citizens from believing the myth that he was born overseas.

It is very hard to say how many Australian journalists have left the profession over the last 10 years.

This is partly because the nature of journalistic work has changed. Many now work aggregating or producing digital content, never leaving their desks.

Institutions such as universities and NGOs are now producing journalistic content, published online, but the people employed to do this task rarely show up in the figures compiled by unions and the Australian Bureau of Statistics, because their employers are not classified as media organisations.

Nevertheless, the big newsrooms have shrunk beyond recognition. This week's announcements were the latest in a 15-year trend. In 2013, industry commentators estimated that more than 3000 Australian journalists had lost their jobs in the previous five years. Since then, there have been further deep cuts, and last week's announcements were merely the latest. In the US, it is estimated that 15 per cent of journalistic jobs disappeared between 2005 and 2009, and the cuts haven't paused since then.

At the same time, and offsetting this, there are new participants in the Australian media. We now have online local versions of the

British Daily Mail, the youth-oriented news and entertainment outlet Buzzfeed, the New York Times, (which has just launched) and the Huffington Post, which operates in partnership with Fairfax. Not least, there is this outlet—an Australian edition of the Guardian.

There are also many small, specialist outlets that exist because the economics of online publishing beat the cost of buying broadcasting licences or printing on bits of dead tree, trucking the papers around the nation and throwing them over the fences.

For the same reasons, almost any large organisation can, if it chooses, use the worldwide web to be a media outlet – though whether the output classes as journalism or public relations is another matter.

Most of the new entrants to the business employ only a few local journalists. The reputable ones struggle to perform miracles each hour with hardly any reporters.

So what does the future hold?

I think it is clear we will have many more smaller newsrooms in the future—including new entrants, non-media organisations touting their wares and the wasted remains of the old businesses.

Some of these newsrooms will operate on the slippery slopes that lie between news, advocacy and advertising.

Some of them will be the fake news factories, devoted to earning an income from spreading clickable, outrageous lies.

If it were only the decline of businesses, we would not need to worry so much. It is rare in history for those who have profited from one technology to go on to dominate the next. Cobb and Co ran the stagecoaches, but not the steam trains.

But it is more serious than the decline of private businesses.

The future is far from clear, but here are some things we can expect to see delivered more quickly than we might think.

First, social media companies will begin to invest in quality content, because otherwise they will lose their audiences.

This is not merely wishful thinking. In China, WeChat, owned by Tencent Corporation, is the dominant social media engine and has functionality that makes Facebook and Twitter look old-fashioned. If you want to know what's coming next in social media, look to China.

As I found on a recent research trip to China, WeChat is investing a lot of money in original journalism. Many of the most interesting journalists in China—including some who have been jailed in the past for their work—are now earning better salaries than those available on party media outlets by freelancing for Tencent, which actively supports and encourages them in multiple ways.

It's counterintuitive, given China's record on freedom of speech, but then the country is changing so fast and is so complex that preconceptions can only be challenged. China might have begun by copying the social media activity of the west, but it has long since outstripped it.

Not that the future dominance of Tencent-like operations is entirely reassuring. WeChat is also a cashless payment system, earning money from transactions. It knows absolutely everything about its users, to a much greater extent than Facebook and Google. It surpasses all previous means of citizen surveillance.

Second, governments will have to take some responsibility for news and information. In Europe and Canada, they are experimenting with methods of helping bolster journalism.

Meanwhile, international research confirms that countries blessed with a strong tradition of publicly funded media are more cohesive, better informed and less polarised. Our own ABC is one of the main reasons we can hope that the trajectory of our democracy will be better than that of the United States.

Lastly, there are citizens. The experience of the last decade tells us that citizen-journalism cannot replace the work done by properly resourced and trained professionals, but it will be a permanent part of the news ecology.

For the foreseeable future, we will be only a few minutes and clicks away from a citizen leaking information, publishing a bare account of a news event or providing a subversive point of view.

In fact, being a responsible consumer, funder and purveyor of news and information is now best understood as one of the many duties of good citizenship. If we can hold firm to that notion, we will come through the crisis.

CHAPTER 2

Does Media Conglomeration Censor the Press?

Conglomerates Run the Media Industry

Ted Turner

Ted Turner is a media executive known for founding the twenty-four-hour news channel CNN. His media conglomerate, Turner Broadcasting System, also operates the channels TBS, TNT, Turner Classic Movies, Cartoon Network, and Adult Swim, which it currently operates as a subsidiary of the telecom giant AT&T.

Fewer and fewer corporations control an ever larger share of what we see in the media. Ted Turner warns that this is a dangerous development for the public, for democracy–even for capitalism itself.

In the late 1960s, when Turner Communications was a business of billboards and radio stations and I was spending much of my energy racing boats, a UHF-TV station came up for sale in Atlanta. It was losing $50,000 U.S. a month and its programmes were viewed by fewer than 5 percent of the market. So I acquired it.

When I moved to buy a second station in Charlotte—this one worse than the first—my accountant quit in protest, and the company's board vetoed the deal. So I mortgaged my house and bought it myself. The Atlanta purchase turned into a Superstation; the Charlotte purchase—when I sold it 10 years later–gave me the capital to launch CNN. Both purchases played a role in revolutionizing television. And neither could happen today.

In the current climate of consolidation in the media industry, independent broadcasters simply don't survive for long. That's why we haven't seen a new generation of people like me or even Rupert Murdoch–independent television upstarts who challenge the big boys and force the whole industry to compete and change. It's not that there aren't entrepreneurs eager to make their names and fortunes in broadcasting if given the chance. If nothing else, the

"My Beef with Big Media," by Ted Turner, Washington Monthly, July/August 2004. Reprinted by permission.

1990s dot-com boom showed that the spirit of entrepreneurship is alive and well in the world today, with plenty of investors willing to put real money into new media ventures.

The difference is that the U.S. government has changed the rules of the game. When I was getting into the television business, lawmakers and the Federal Communications Commission (FCC) took seriously the commission's mandate to promote diversity, localism, and competition in the media marketplace. They wanted to make sure that the big, established networks—CBS, ABC, NBC—wouldn't forever dominate what the American public could watch on TV. They wanted independent television producers to thrive. They wanted more people to be able to own TV stations. They believed in the value of competition. When the FCC had received a glut of applications for new television stations after World War II, the agency set aside dozens of channels on the new UHF spectrum so independents could get a foothold in television. That helped me get my start 35 years ago.

But that was then.

Today, media companies are more concentrated than at any time over the past 40 years, thanks to a continual loosening of ownership rules by the FCC. Media giants now own not only broadcast networks and local stations; they also own the cable companies and the studios that produce most of the programming. To get a flavour of how consolidated the industry has become, consider this: In 1990, the major broadcast networks—ABC, CBS, NBC, and Fox—fully or partially owned just 12.5 percent of the new television series they aired; the rest were from independent producers. By 2000, it was 56.3 percent. Just two years later, it had surged to 77.5 percent.

In this environment, most independent media firms either get gobbled up by one of the big companies or driven out of business altogether. Yet instead of balancing the rules to give independent broadcasters a fair chance in the market, Washington continues to tilt the playing field to favour the biggest players.

In the media, as in any industry, big corporations play a vital role, but so do small, emerging ones. When you lose small businesses, you lose big ideas. People who own their own businesses are independent thinkers. They know they can't compete by imitating the big guys—they have to innovate. They are quicker to seize on new technologies and new product ideas. They steal market share from the big companies, spurring them to adopt new approaches. This process promotes competition, which leads to higher quality, more jobs and greater wealth. It's called capitalism.

But without the proper rules, healthy capitalist markets turn into sluggish oligopolies—and that is what's happening in media today. Large corporations are more profit-focused and risk-averse than ever before. The moguls behind the mergers are acting in their corporate interests and playing by the rules. We just shouldn't accept those rules. They make sense for a corporation. But for a society, it's like over-fishing the oceans. When the independent businesses are gone, where will the new ideas come from? We have to do more than keep media giants from growing larger; they're already too big. We need a new set of rules that will break these huge companies into smaller ones.

Throughout the 1990s, media mergers were celebrated in the press and otherwise ignored by the American public. So, it was easy to assume that media consolidation was neither controversial nor problematic. But then a funny thing happened. In the summer of 2003, the FCC proposed changes favouring even more consolidation—raising the national audience-reach cap from 35 percent to 45 percent; allowing corporations to own a newspaper and a TV station in the same market; and permitting corporations to own three TV stations in the largest markets, up from two, and two stations in medium-sized markets, up from one.

Unexpectedly, the public rebelled. Hundreds of thousands of citizens complained to the FCC. Groups ranging from the National Organization for Women to the National Rifle Association demanded that Congress reverse the ruling. And lawmakers finally took action, pushing the national audience cap back down to 35, until—under strong White House pressure—it was revised back up to 39 percent. Last June, the U.S. Court of Appeals threw out the rules that would have allowed corporations to own more television and radio stations in a single market.

The FCC defends its actions by saying that we have more media choices than ever before. But only a few corporations decide what we can choose. That is not choice. **That's like a dictator deciding what candidates are allowed to stand for parliamentary elections**, and then claiming that the people choose their leaders. The loss of independent operators hurts both the media business and its citizen-customers. When they disappear, the emphasis in the media shifts from taking risks to raking in profits. When that happens, quality suffers, local culture suffers and democracy itself suffers. Top managers in these huge media conglomerates run their companies for the short term. Media mega-mergers inevitably lead to an overemphasis on short-term earnings.

You can see this overemphasis in the spread of reality television. Shows like Fear Factor cost little to produce—there are no actors to pay and no sets to maintain—and they get big ratings. Thus, American television has moved away from expensive sitcoms and on to cheap thrills. We've gone from Father Knows Best to Who Wants to Marry My Dad?, and from My Three Sons to My Big Fat Obnoxious Fiancé.

Consolidation also means a decline in the local focus of both news and programming. After analyzing 23,000 stories on 172 news programmes over five years, the Project for Excellence in Journalism found that big media news organizations relied more on syndicated feeds and were more likely to air national stories with no local connection than smaller ones. That's not surprising. Local coverage is expensive, and will usually be sacrificed in the quest for short-term earnings.

Loss of local content also undercuts the public-service mission of the media, and this can have dangerous consequences. In early 2002, when a freight train derailed near Minot, N.D., releasing a cloud of anhydrous ammonia over the town, police tried to call local radio stations, six of which are owned by radio mammoth Clear Channel Communications. According to news reports, it took over an hour to reach anyone at the stations to put an alert on the air. No one was answering the phone because the programming for all six stations was being beamed from Clear Channel headquarters in San Antonio, Texas–some 1,600 miles away. By the next day, 300 people had been hospitalized, many partially blinded by the ammonia. Pets and livestock died.

Consolidation has given big media companies new power over what is said not just on the air, but off it as well. Cumulus Media banned the band Dixie Chicks on its 42 country music stations for 30 days after lead singer Natalie Maines criticized President Bush for the war in Iraq. It's hard to imagine Cumulus would have been so bold if its listeners had more of a choice in country music stations.

And Disney recently provoked an uproar when it prevented its subsidiary Miramax from distributing Michael Moore's film Fahrenheit 9/11. As a senior Disney executive told The New York Times: "It's not in the interest of any major corporation to be dragged into a highly charged partisan political battle." Follow the logic, and you can see what lies ahead: if the only media companies are major corporations, controversial and dissenting views may not be aired at all.

This is a fight about freedom—the freedom of independent entrepreneurs to start and run a media business, and the freedom of citizens to get news, information, and entertainment from a wide variety of sources, at least some of which are truly independent and not run by people making decisions based on quarterly earnings reports. No one should underestimate the danger. Big media companies want to eliminate all ownership limits. With the removal of these limits, immense media power will pass into the hands of a very few corporations and individuals.

What will programming be like when it's produced for no other purpose than profit? What will news be like when there are no independent news organizations to go after stories the big corporations avoid? Who really wants to find out? Safeguarding the welfare of the public cannot be the first concern of a large publicly traded media company. Its job is to seek profits. But if the government writes the rules in a way that encourages entry into the market of entrepreneurs—men and women with big dreams, new ideas, and a willingness to take long-term risks—the economy will be stronger, and the country will be better off.

Media companies have grown so large and powerful, and their dominance has become so detrimental to the survival of small, emerging companies, that there remains only one alternative: bust up the big conglomerates. We've done this before: to the railroad monopolies in the first part of the twentieth century, to phone companies more recently. Breaking up the media conglomerates may seem like an impossible task when their grip on the policy-making process in Washington seems so sure. But the public's broad and bipartisan rebellion against the FCC's pro-consolidation decisions suggests something different. Politically, big media may again be on the wrong side of history—and up against a country unwilling to lose its independents.

Media Conglomeration Is a Threat to Democracy

Michael Corcoran

Michael Corcoran is a Boston-based writer who has written for the Boston Globe, *the* Nation, *and the* Christian Science Monitor, *as well as the news nonprofit* Truthout.

Wall Street's sinister influence on the political process has, rightly, been a major topic during this presidential campaign. But, history has taught us that the role that the media industry plays in Washington poses a comparable threat to our democracy. Yet, this is a topic rarely discussed by the dominant media, or on the campaign trail.

But now is a good time to discuss our growing media crises. Twenty years ago this week, President Bill Clinton signed the Telecommunications Act of 1996. The act, signed into law on February 8, 1996, was "essentially bought and paid for by corporate media lobbies," as Fairness and Accuracy in Reporting (FAIR) described it, and radically "opened the floodgates on mergers."

The negative impact of the law cannot be overstated. The law, which was the first major reform of telecommunications policy since 1934, according to media scholar Robert McChesney, "is widely considered to be one of the three or four most important federal laws of this generation." The act dramatically reduced important Federal Communications Commission (FCC) regulations on cross ownership, and allowed giant corporations to buy up thousands of media outlets across the country, increasing their monopoly on the flow of information in the United States and around the world.

"Democracy in Peril: Twenty Years of Media Consolidation Under the Telecommunications Act," by Michael Corcoran, Truthout, February 11, 2016. Reprinted by permission.

"Never have so many been held incommunicado by so few," said Eduardo Galeano, the Latin American journalist, in response to the act.

Twenty years later the devastating impact of the legislation is undeniable: About 90 percent of the country's major media companies are owned by six corporations. Bill Clinton's legacy in empowering the consolidation of corporate media is right up there with the North American Free Trade Agreement (NAFTA) and welfare reform, as being among the most tragic and destructive policies of his administration.

The Telecommunications Act of 1996 is not merely a regrettable part of history. It serves as a stern warning about what is at stake in the future. In a media world that is going through a massive transformation, media companies have dramatically increased efforts to wield influence in Washington, with a massive lobbying presence and a steady dose of campaign donations to politicians in both parties—with the goal of allowing more consolidation, and privatizing and commodifying the internet.

This issue has not been central in the 2016 presidential election. But it is deeply concerning that, of all the presidential candidates running in 2016, the Big Media lobby has chosen to back Hillary Clinton. Media industry giants have donated way more to her than any other candidate in the race, according to data from the Center for Responsive Politics. In light of this, we must be mindful of the media reform challenges we face in the present, as we try to prevent the type of damage to our democracy that was caused by the passing of this unfortunate law.

A Threat to Democracy: The Telecommunications Act and Media Consolidation

When President Bill Clinton signed the Telecommunications Act into law, he did so with great fanfare. The bill, which was lobbied for in great numbers by the communications and media industry, was sadly a bipartisan misadventure—only 3 percent of

Congress voted against the bill: five senators and 16 members of the House, including then-Rep. Bernie Sanders.

At the time, President Clinton touted the law as "truly revolutionary legislation … that really embodies what we ought to be about as a country." House Speaker Newt Gingrich boasted of projected consumer savings and private job growth. Rep. John Dingell (D-Michigan) "thanked God" for the bill that would "make this country the best served, the best educated and the most successful country … in all areas of communications."

Despite all of these glowing words, the consequences of the bill were disastrous. The act "fueled a consolidation so profound that even insiders are surprised by its magnitude," said one trade publication, according to Robert McChesney, in his book, *Rich Media, Poor Democracy: Communication Politics in Dubious Times.*

"Before the ink was even dry on the 1996 Act," wrote S. Derek Turner, research director of Free Press, in a 2009 report proposing a national broadband strategy, "the powerful media and telecommunications giants and their army of overpaid lobbyists went straight to work obstructing and undermining the competition the new law was intended to create."

Media consolidation was already an extremely pressing concern long before 1996. In 1983, Ben Bagdikian published his groundbreaking book, *The Media Monopoly*, which revealed that just 50 corporations owned 90 percent of the media. That number gradually dwindled over the coming 13 years and was accelerated by the Telecommunications Act. This has led us to the aforementioned crisis where more than 90 percent of the mediais owned by just six companies: Viacom, News Corporation, Comcast, CBS, Time Warner and Disney.

Radio has seen an equally appalling consolidation, which has been horrendous for both news media and music. In 1995, before the Telecommunications Act was passed, companies were not allowed to own more than 40 radio stations. "Since passage of the 1996 Telecommunications Act, Clear Channel [now called iHeartMedia] has grown from 40 stations to 1,240 stations

—30 times more than congressional regulation previously allowed," according to a report from the Future of Music Coalition.

Local newspapers, too, have been stung by these deregulations. Gannett, for instance, owns more than 1,000 newspapers and 600 print periodicals. Layoffs have been the norm for the company, including at USA Today, the paper with the largest circulation in the country, where layoffs were described as a "total bloodbath" in the American Journalism Review.

Save the Internet: The Next Big Media Battle

There was a lot at stake when media companies lobbied for reform in 1996. There is just as much at stake today in the battle for a free and open press. Not only have big media companies continued to push for more consolidation and mergers, but they are also seeking to commodify and privatize the internet. This has become a major concern for advocates of "net neutrality," who want to "save the internet," and ensure it is protected as a public utility with equal access for everybody. An FCC ruling in February 2015 has protected the internet for now, but as Free Press warns, the internet is still "in danger."

"Net neutrality has made the internet an unrivaled space for free speech, civic participation, innovation and opportunity. Net neutrality prohibits online discrimination and gives any individual, organization or company the same chance to share their ideas and find an audience," explains Free Press's website, Save the Internet. "Companies like Comcast and Verizon aren't used to losing in Washington, and they'll do everything they can to knock down the Title II protections the FCC approved on Feb. 26, 2015."

The organization is right to be concerned. One reason for the passage of the Telecommunications Act of 1996, as McChesney wrote in 1997, was the sheer power that the media and communications industry has in Washington. "Both the Democratic and Republican parties have strong ties to the large communication firms and industries, and the communication lobbies are among the most feared, respected and well-endowed of all that seek favors on Capitol Hill."

Today that power and influence has only increased. "From 2002-2008, the industry increased its spending on lobbying efforts every year," reports the Center for Responsive Politics. "The streak snapped when the Great Recession set in and most clients cut back on their DC efforts, and then reversed again in 2013. In 2014, cable and satellite providers spent nearly $8.1 [million] on lobbying."

Big Media's Relationship With Hillary Clinton

What is most revealing when analyzing the donation patterns of these industries in the data from the Center for Responsive Politics —be it cable television, print and periodicals, radio or telecom services—is that Hillary Clinton is, by far, the largest recipient of donations of any candidate in the 2016 election in either party. In fact, of all the top industries that have donated to Clinton, the TV/movies/music category ranks behind only the securities and investments category. (This data is from reports filed on January 31, 2016, according to the Center for Responsive Politics.)

More troubling is that these filings come on the heels of a report from Politico that the Clinton Foundation has received donations, some of them very large, from most of all the major media companies directly: Viacom, News Corporation, Reuters, NBCUniversal, Newsmax, Time Warner, Mort Zuckerman (owner of US News &World Report and the New York Daily News), Comcast, AOL Huffington Post Media and Robert Allbritton (owner of Politico). George Stephanopoulos, one of ABC News' most visible journalist and a former staffer for President Clinton, has also been under scrutiny for not disclosing a $75,000 donation to the foundation.

Of course, the Clinton Foundation is not a political campaign and does some philanthropic work. So while this all might be legal, it is extremely unsettling, especially in tandem with all the campaign donations Hillary Clinton has received from the major players in this industry.

In March 2015, for instance, a Comcast executive held a $50,000 per plate fundraiser for Clinton's super PAC. "Comcast NBCUniversal operates in 39 states and has 130,000 employees across the country," said company spokeswoman Sena Fitzmaurice at the time. "It is important for our customers, our employees and our shareholders that we participate in the political process."

Of course, media companies don't just donate to Clinton, but also to members of Congress from both parties. Further, as the Center for Responsive Politics reports, the FCC is filled with "revolving-door" employees, who have been switching back and forth between government work and lobbying for Comcast.

Their aggressiveness in Washington makes them a dangerous enemy in the fight for free and democratic media. In this environment, it should come as no surprise that the position of FCC chairman is typically held by a former lobbyist for the cable industry, such as Tom Wheeler, the current chairman, who was once president of the National Cable and Telecommunications Association, a major opponent of net neutrality.

And while it is good news that Clinton has come out in favor of net neutrality, it is a reasonable fear that she could change her views once elected, especially given her relationship with Big Media. It would not be the first time a president has changed a view after being elected, as we learned when Barack Obama embraced a mandate in health care, or when George H.W. Bush raised taxes, despite his infamous promise that he never would.

It is important to note that, whatever her relationship with the telecommunications industry, it is not fair to blame Hillary Clinton for the Telecommunications Act of 1996. As first lady, Clinton was not in charge of telecommunications policy and there doesn't appear to be evidence she played a role in constructing or fighting for the law in the White House. In fact, 20 years later, it is difficult to find any public statements from Hillary Clinton expressing her opinion about the law or its impacts. She did address a question at the 2012 YearlyKos convention about the Telecommunications Act. Her response, however, did little to clarify her views on the subject. She said:

> You'll have to ask [then-Vice President] Al Gore. We've had a lot of media consolidation. We've had some good competition. We have a lot that we need to do to begin to create a more competitive framework. Al was very involved in designing and pushing that through—he is an expert; I am not … We've got to take a hard look at this and I don't want to say something I may not really support. So I have to look at that proposal.

Clinton is now, however, deep into a presidential run and could well be responsible for appointing the head of the FCC. She owes it to voters to describe her views on the Telecommunications Act, and on media consolidation more broadly, in a way that goes beyond advising Americans to "go ask Al Gore."

Why Media Reform Matters

When McChesney observed that the communications lobby was "among the most feared, respected and well-endowed of all" groups in Washington, he also pointed out one of the great challenges about trying to fight Big Media.

"[The] only grounds for political independence in this case," he wrote about the debate over the Telecommunications Act, "would be if there were an informed and mobilized citizenry ready to do battle for alternative policies. But where would citizens get informed?"

In other words, how can we have a real debate about media issues, when we depend on that very media to provide a platform for this debate? It is no surprise, for instance, that the media largely ignored the impact of *Citizens United* after the Supreme Court decision helped media companies generate record profits due to a new mass of political ads. "Super PACs may be bad for America, but they're very good for CBS," said CBS president Les Moonves, in a rare moment of candor at an entertainment conference in 2012.

This catch-22 is indeed one of the great difficulties about fighting for a vibrant media and a healthy democracy. But it is a challenge advocates of free media must embrace. Supporting independent media is one important way to help bring light to issues the corporate media ignores.

Media reform is the issue that affects all other issues. As the impact of the Telecommunications Act of 1996 has shown, democracy suffers when almost all media in the nation is owned by massive conglomerates. In this reality, no issue the left cares about—the environment, criminal legal reform or health care—will get a fair shake in the national debate.

Media Conglomerates Tell Their Journalists What They Can and Cannot Say

Glenn Greenwald

Glenn Greenwald is a journalist whose investigation of the United States and British global surveillance programs won the Pulitzer Prize in 2014. He is a founding editor of the Intercept.

I want to return to the subject of GE's silencing of Keith Olbermann both because there are new facts I've obtained that shed light on what happened here and because this is one of the most blatant examples yet of pernicious corporate control over America's journalism. The most striking aspect of this episode is that GE isn't even bothering any longer to deny the fact that they exert control over MSNBC's journalism. They've brazenly dispensed with the long-held fiction of the sanctity of journalistic independence from interference by the corporate parents that own America's largest news organizations.

Instead, GE is now openly and proudly boasting of their editorial control over the news organizations they own, and publicly rubbing it in the faces of NBC News journalists that they're subservient to GE's corporate agenda. Look at this smug, creepy quote from GE executive spokesman Gary Sheffer explaining in *The New York Times* why GE issued its gag order preventing Olbermann from criticizing Fox and O'Reilly, all but mocking NBC and MSNBC journalists as nothing more than GE's office of corporate spokespeople:

> "We all recognize that a certain level of civility needed to be introduced into the public discussion," Gary Sheffer, a spokesman for G.E., said this week. "We're happy that has happened."

Why is GE even speaking for MSNBC's editorial decisions at all? Needless to say, GE doesn't care in the slightest about "civility"

"The scope—and dangers—of GE's control of NBC and MSNBC," by Glenn Greenwald, Salon Media Group, Inc., August 3, 2009. Reprinted by permission.

in general. Mika Brzezinski can spout that people who dislike Sarah Palin aren't "real Americans" and Chris Matthews can say about George Bush that "everybody sort of likes the president, except for the real whack-jobs," and GE executives won't (and didn't) bat an eye. What they mean by "civility" is: "thou shalt not criticize anyone who can harm GE's business interests or who will report on our actions." Thus: *GE's journalists will stop reporting critically on Fox and its top assets because Fox can expose actions of GE that we want to keep concealed.*

Does anyone need it explained to them why it is so dangerous and destructive to have our political debates controlled by GE executives, sitting in their offices censoring the journalism of our leading media outlets in the name of "civility," code for: you will respect those who can harm us? Our entire political culture is already designed to ensure corporate control of our political institutions. Their lobbyists literally write the laws enacted by Congress and control their implementation. The reason the journalism industry insisted for so long on the ludicrous fiction that corporate parents never violated the sanctity of journalistic independence is precisely because everyone understood why that would be so dangerous. Apparently, they no longer feel a need to maintain that fiction.

GE's control over two major American news outlets— NBC, which uses our public airways, and MSNBC—is inherently dangerous even without evidence of its editorial interference. GE's corporate interests in the outcome of our political process is vast and impossible to overstate. In 2006, *The Boston Globe* reported:

> General Electric Co. spent $21.5 million last year trying to influence the US government, the most of any corporation, as total lobbying costs rose even as Congress began looking at ways to rein in such activities.

GE's relationship with the U.S. Government is a vital aspect of its business:

Federal contracts for General Electric, based in Fairfield, Conn., rose to $3.8 billion during the two years ending Sept. 30, 2004, the last period for which figures are available.

In June of this year, in an article headlined "General Electric is Once Again the Lobbying Champion," *The Washington Times* reported:

> General Electric spent more on lobbying in this year's first quarter than any other company, newly filed federal lobbying reports show. The company shelled out $7.2 million for lobbyists in April, May, and June—that's $160,000 each day Congress was in session.
>
> The only other company to spend more than $6 million was Chevron, and GE almost equaled the Chamber of Commerce's lobbying budget.
>
> GE is perennially atop this list, according to the Center for Responsive Politics. The company has spent $187 million on lobbying over the past decade, 44% more than runner-up Northrup Grumman.
>
> Why? Because no other company is so intimately tied up with government—a dynamic that has only intensified in the Obama administration.

And just today, by sweet coincidence, Fred Hiatt turned over his *Washington Post* Editorial Page to GE CEO Jeffrey Immelt, along with Silicon Valley investor John Doerr, to argue that the U.S. government must spend more on wind power technology. Why? Because GE is the only American company in the world's top six largest wind technology manufacturers and had a major stake in the use of such technology by governments. GE constantly manipulates our political process and institutions for its own self-interest. And it now manipulates our political debates, through its control over our leading news outlets, for the same purposes. Who wouldn't be seriously disturbed by GE's control over substantial aspects of America's journalism?

Critically, GE's decree to silence Olbermann is only the most recent incident of GE's interference with the journalism decisions of NBC and MSNBC—interference that has been triggering increasing (though largely impotent) anger and resentment among NBC employees. Much of the tension goes back to last year when GE executives directed MSNBC to remove Olbermann and Chris Matthews as election show anchors, according to an MSNBC source with management responsibilities, who insisted on anonymity because he is divulging information adverse to his bosses and because having his name attached to these leaks would jeopardize his job security (exactly the circumstances I've always argued renders anonymity appropriate).

Last year's GE/MSNBC controversy occurred because the McCain campaign—which had been constantly complaining about MSNBC—threatened to pull out of a presidential debate to be hosted by NBC's Tom Brokaw if Olbermann and Matthews continued anchoring election coverage. Brokaw then went to GE 's CEO Jeffrey Immelt—not to NBC executives—to demand that Olbermann and Matthews be removed as anchors in order to preserve his prestigious status as debate moderator. In fact, as *The New York Observer* reported at the time, Andrea Mitchell also wanted Olbermann and Matthews removed as anchors and thus raised the issue at a dinner for a handful of NBC stars hosted by Immelt.

Though MSNBC denied it at the time, it was GE—just as they're doing now in barring Olbermann from talking about O'Reilly—which capitulated to the Right's demands by instructing MSNBC to remove Olbermann and Matthews as election anchors. When it happened, I wrote about the removal of Olbermann/Matthews as anchors under the headline: "The Right dictates MSNBC's programming decisions."

That it is GE which controls the editorial decisions of NBC and MSNBC is an open secret in Washington. Just today, *The Washington Post's* Howard Kurtz wrote about Obama Chief of Staff Rahm Emanuel's actions after learning that the news networks were reluctant to broadcast Obama's most recent press conference on health care. Did Emanuel attempt to pressure NBC executives to capitulate to White House demands to broadcast that event? No; he obviously knew who really makes editorial decisions for those networks:

> In the days before President Obama's last news conference, as the networks weighed whether to give up a chunk of their precious prime time, Rahm Emanuel went straight to the top.
>
> Rather than calling ABC, the White House chief of staff phoned Bob Iger, chief executive of parent company Disney. Instead of contacting NBC, Emanuel went to Jeffrey Immelt, the chief executive of General Electric. He also spoke with Les Moonves, the chief executive of CBS, the company spun off from Viacom.

Apparently, Rahm Emanuel isn't confused about who the real bosses are at America's major news networks. Although Kurtz claims that Immelt—who was named by Obama as a member of his Economics Advisory Board—told Emanuel that this would be a decision for NBC's Jeff Zucker to make, all networks ultimately acceded to Emanuel's demands, directed to the CEOs of the parent corporations, and broadcast Obama's press conference, just as the White House demanded they do.

GE—deeply concerned about Fox's reporting of its actions in Iran and other potential disclosures—has long been discussing a *quid pro quo* with Rupert Murdoch, whereby GE would give in to O'Reilly's demands that Olbermann be barred from criticizing him in exchange for O'Reilly's agreement to cease reporting on GE's dubious corporate activities. More than a year ago, Howard Kurtz noted:

> Asked about O'Reilly's motivation [in criticizing GE], [GE's] Sheffer said that executives at Murdoch's News Corp. "tell us if the attacks on O'Reilly end, the attacks on GE will end. They've had conversations with our news executives saying, 'If you stop, we'll stop' " . . . .
>
> Early last year, the sources say, [NBC President Steve] Capus called [Fox's Roger] Ailes to say that O'Reilly had gone over the line with reckless attacks on Engel. But, the sources recounted,

Ailes said he agreed that NBC was against the war and had aligned itself with Olbermann's mockery. Capus, he said, had the power to shut down the situation by telling Olbermann to back off.

Immelt was essentially being blackmailed by News Corp.: we will continue to report on GE's corporate activities unless you bar Keith Olbermann from criticizing Fox and O'Reilly. And now, Immelt has succumbed to those threats and ordered Olbermann to cease reporting on Fox. There is simply no doubt—none—that this happened. That is the reason that O'Reilly's name has not passed Olbermann's lips since June 1—because GE, petrified of further reporting by Fox of its corporate activities, has barred Olbermann from doing so. Another source who regularly appears on MSNBC—demanding anonymity for fear of jeopardizing further appearances—was recently told by a segment producer that explicit mentions of Fox News were prohibited.

According to the above-referenced MSNBC management source, there has been talk among MSNBC employees ever since the GE edict was issued about ways to protest it and to stand up for their journalistic freedom. Many are afraid that their journalistic reputations will suffer by being so publicly humiliated by GE, while others are concerned that they are no longer allowed to alienate the Right since GE has made clear that they will censor editorial content and publicy embarrass even highly profitable stars like Olbermann whenever the Right targets GE with grievances over NBC's reporting. Since the GE/Olbermann decree was issued, everything has been discussed at MSNBC from joint defiance of this edict to mini-strikes in the form of prolonged vacations and absences. Although Olbermann did take an unusually long vacation in the ratings-important month of July, there is little evidence yet that any genuine pushback has occurred or has been effective.

It's worth underscoring that these incidents of overt GE control over NBC and MSNBC are merely the ones that have been publicly described (David Sirota, who first raised concerns about corporate flack Richard Wolffe's guest-hosting *Countdown*, today documents similar examples of corporate interference at other networks). It is highly likely there are other undisclosed examples at NBC, but more important, corporate employees don't need to be told what their bosses want. They know without being told. GE's business vitally depends on favorable relationships with the Government, and they have signaled that they are unwilling to alienate the Right generally or News Corp. and Fox News specifically. It takes no effort to see how profoundly those corporate interests affect the "journalism" of NBC and MSNBC. Given GE's insistence that NBC advance its corporate agenda, do you think Brian Williams, earning $10 million a year, would ever do anything contrary to GE's corporate interests?

If corporations that own media outlets engage in *quid pro quos* to prevent critical reporting about one another, then large corporations—which own the Congress and control regulatory agencies—have no checks imposed on them at all. By law, the "public airwaves" are required to be used for the "public interest." Clearly, NBC News—which depends on use of the public airwaves—is used for GE's interests. They assume that they don't need to hide this any longer because nobody is willing to do anything about it.

A Controlled Press Is a Bad Press

Mike Floorwalker

Mike Floorwalker is a professional freelance writer and video producer whose work has appeared in Listverse, Cracked, and Looper.

Passed in 1996 under President Bill Clinton, the Telecommunications Act has resulted in large-scale deregulation of the entire US media industry, removing many limitations on the number of different media outlets that can be owed by a single company. Today, six corporations control 90 percent of all of the media output in the United States. As we will see, this has affected the quality, variety, and accessibility of US media in a number of ways.

Lack of Competition Drives Up Costs

It is a well-known economic principle that competition within an industry tends to drive prices down, so it stands to reason that the fewer providers there are for a product or service, the more prices will stagnate or rise. For an example of this in the telecommunications industry, look no further than Comcast—the nation's largest cable television provider and also one of the six aforementioned corporations that control most of the output across all media.

Cable costs have continued to rise in large part because of retransmission fees, which the large broadcasting corporations must pay to smaller broadcasters to air their content. Said content is free to anyone with an antenna, but these fees, along with no incentive to price services competitively, have helped lead to ever-escalating cable bills, with no end in sight.

"10 Ways Mass Media Ownership Hurts The Public," by Mike Floorwalker, Listverse Ltd, October 6, 2016. Reprinted by permission.

The sheer size of these corporations encourages them to cooperate, rather than compete, with each other. As ex-Viacom president Mel Karmazin put it, "You find it very difficult to go to war with one piece of Viacom without going to war with all of Viacom." This means that pricing structures are largely agreed upon between "competing" providers.

Threat to Net Neutrality

While the FCC's 2015 ruling declaring the Internet a public utility was an important victory, there are still many battles ahead for net neutrality—the idea that Internet service providers should not favor one content provider over another. As media conglomerates grow larger and richer, they are better able to leverage their resources for lobbying, and it has long been a goal of these corporations to privatize the Internet.

Since 2002, the amount of money spent by large telecom companies on lobbying Congress has steadily increased. Also, nearly all major media companies contribute extensively to presidential campaigns. Since the Internet allows literally anyone to provide the same type of content provided by the large corporations, often for free, it seems unlikely that this type of spending is being done with no expectation of a return on the investment.

In addition to the threat of competition, the large telecom companies have a simple reason for their desire for privatization—more efficient targeted advertising, a highly questionable benefit to the consumer but an obvious benefit to advertisers and service providers.

Homogenization of Content

In the early 2000s, many radio listeners noticed that their local stations had changed formats and were now being promoted as "Jack FM," a "play what we want" format that played hits from every decade since the 1960s. The branding, and its programming, is licensed by one company to dozens of outlets in four different countries.

This helps to illustrate the problem of content becoming less diversified, which has been particularly pronounced in radio. One company, iHeart Media (formerly known as Clear Channel) has risen to dominate US radio programming. Today, it owns over 850 radio stations, simulcasting preselected and prerecorded content to all of them. Not only does this reduce the number of listening options available over public airwaves, but it also undercuts opportunities for musicians, who are forced to consider the mandates of this one corporation if they want any hope of procuring airtime.

Less Focus on Local Programming

When a smaller outlet is acquired by a media conglomerate, the corporation's focus is primarily on turning a quick profit to justify the purchase. This stifles innovation and also has the side effect of discouraging the recently acquired stations from continuing to focus on local programming.

As mentioned previously, it makes little sense to pay retransmission fees to broadcast content that consumers can receive over the airwaves for free. Piped-in, self-produced content is far more economically viable, and even the FCC has recently been forced to admit that this system is due for an overhaul. The effect, especially in larger markets, has been a slow dwindling of local news as well as community-oriented and educational programming.

Fewer Viewpoints

It is an unfortunate but undeniable fact that most major corporations do not often remain politically or socially neutral. Under US law, corporations have a number of options for helping to advance or stifle political or social agendas. Media conglomerates have a potent and cost-effective weapon of their own—the ability to promote favorable agendas or silence dissenting ones using their control over their outlets.

A high-profile example of this remains relevant years after the fact: In 2003, the members of country-rock band The Dixie Chicks criticized the policies of then-president George W. Bush during a concert. Subsequently, Cox Radio and Cumulus Media ordered all of their hundreds of affiliated stations to refrain from playing the band's music—a ban from which the band never recovered.

Several recent studies have suggested that the interests of women and ethnic minorities have been served poorly by this concentration of ownership. It was found that large media companies cater mostly to white, male audiences, while ownership of the actual outlets by women and minorities stands at less than four percent.

Media Bias

Also problematic is that large corporations tend to diversify their interests, meaning that most media corporations have ties to other industries. Many of these industries, such as logging, oil extraction, real estate, and utilities, depend heavily on a positive public perception, and it's easy to see the potential conflicts of interest that can emerge.

This effect can be hard to pin down, as the ownership structures of media companies are rarely transparent. Such companies are not required to disclose data on investors or often even who holds actual ownership stakes in them. They also aren't required to disclose their sources of income.

Relationships with advertisers can exacerbate this effect. Famed political activist Noam Chomsky has pointed out that large media companies tend to shape their content to best attract potential advertisers and that the largest of these advertisers often have editorial input over content.

Freedom of the Press

The combined effect of these competing influences is an environment in which unfettered freedom of the press is directly threatened. For evidence of this, look no further than the country whose media most closely resembles the model toward which the US is moving—Russia.

While the Russian government does not technically own all of the country's media outlets, the control that it exerts over content is nearly total. The result is a largely impotent media that speaks with one carefully cultured voice, in which dissenting viewpoints are never allowed to see the light of day, much less receive serious discussion.

While the US isn't there yet, the FCC's continued support of policies which encourage further consolidation isn't very encouraging. As previously mentioned, US law provides many loopholes through which corporations are allowed to throw almost unlimited funds behind political candidates or causes—encouraging and deepening the cozy relationships between media corporations and legislators.

Censorship

While most tend to think of censorship as an outright ban on certain information by those within the government, the reality is far less simple. Media outlets routinely engage in self-censorship, some of which is admirable, such as refusal to release the names of sexual assault victims. Consider, however, that information is a commodity, and the government is often a primary source of information.

Media outlets need to have the most current information to remain relevant and are therefore dependent on government agencies for a great deal of their content. This has an editorial "chilling effect"—a reluctance to report stories which may, for example, cast the current war effort in an unfavorable light or call government policies into question. This has had a devastating effect on both the quality and objectivity of the press as well as the public's perception of it.

Public Distrust

While the US media is presenting an increasingly narrow spectrum of viewpoints, the range of information available on the Internet has exploded. Of course, not all of this is good information, but it has resulted in an unprecedented amount of cognitive dissonance among a public which is presented with information from the media that does not line up with what they believe to be true.

A recent study by the American Press Institute illustrates this dramatically. In a survey of over 2,000 adults, a mere six percent professed to have a "great deal of confidence" in the media, while 41 percent described themselves as having "hardly any confidence." This general perception of untrustworthiness has grown steadily in the last two decades.

Along with the other above factors, this may be the death knell of what was once considered to be the single most important function of the press in the United States.

Decline Of the 'Fourth Estate'

The US press was originally intended to act as an unofficial fourth branch of government—a "Fourth Estate," meant to keep the other three branches honest and the public informed as to what was being done in their name. In perhaps the most shining example of the press acting in this capacity, a pair of *Washington Post* reporters in the early 1970s followed a seemingly minor story of a break-in at the Democratic National Headquarters all the way to the office of the president, resulting in the impeachment and eventual resignation of Richard M. Nixon.

It is difficult to imagine a similar scenario playing out today. Consolidated ownership of outlets, combined with the relationships of these corporations among each other and government entities, are beginning to result in a press which is far more focused on the "national interest" than on the public interest. Continued consolidation can only further erode this vital function—and open the door yet further to a government that is no longer beholden to the will of its people.

Large Media Companies Can Keep News Outlets Alive

Kyle Pope

Kyle Pope is the editor in chief of the Columbia Journalism Review, *a magazine published by Columbia University's Graduate School of Journalism.*

I s it an underhanded compliment to be called the most innovative company in the newspaper business?

The Washington Post will happily take it. In the three years since Amazon's Jeff Bezos bought the Post for $250 million—now seen as a steal for one of the great brands in publishing—the Post has reinvented itself with digital speed. Its Web traffic has doubled since Bezos arrived, and it far outstrips *The New York Times* (and even BuzzFeed) in the number of online posts its reporters file every day. So successful has the Post become in the digital game that it now licenses its content management system to other news outlets, a business that could generate $100 million a year.

It is a moment to savor for a once-iconic family business that has spent much of the last decade in retreat. When Bezos bought the Post in 2013, its news franchise had been decimated by Politico (which will soon celebrate its 10th anniversary); it had lost its editor; and its digital business had four years earlier joined the mothership from an office in Arlington.

Today, the office has the feel of a tech startup well-blessed by the VC gods. Video screens scrolling Web analytics hang above the newsroom. Reporters roam the place carrying laptops.

The *Post*'s turnaround, in a terrible period for newspapers, has made Martin Baron, its editor, a journalism rock star (Pulitzer Prize, dominating coverage of the 2016 election, portrayal by Liev Schreiber in an Oscar-winning movie). But it has also raised the

"Revolution at The Washington Post," by Kyle Pope, Columbia Journalism Review, Fall/Winter 2016. Reprinted by permission.

profile of the paper's tech team, who have become stars in their own right on the digital-media conference circuit. If a paper like the *Post* can right itself digitally, perhaps there's hope for everyone else.

There most certainly could be, if everyone else were owned by a billionaire who sees today's media game as analogous to the internet circa 1999, essentially a land grab open to whomever can spend the most money and move the fastest to grab the biggest market share. That is the story of the rise of Amazon.com, and Bezos is applying many of those same lessons to the *Post*. (Along with an obsession with Web traffic and engagement metrics, which are much more important internally than whether the paper makes any money.)

The *Post*, working with Google, also has moved aggressively to make its mobile site load stories faster, on the assumption (anathema to reporters) that readers will choose news outlets based in part on how fast they are. Another tool at the company, for Web scheduling, automatically hounds reporters missing their deadlines.

The pair Bezos has chosen to pull off all of this could not be more of an odd work couple. Shailesh Prakash, the *Post*'s chief information officer, is an old-school technologist, with stints at Microsoft and Netscape, and no experience in media before joining the *Post* five years ago. He is as corporate (khakis and button-down shirt) and conventional, at least in appearance, as his technology partner at the *Post* is not.

Joey Marburger, the paper's director of product, was dubbed the *Post*'s "punk rock star" by Digiday.com, no doubt due to the ear studs and the fact that he played bass in a punk band in high school. Marburger is the journalist of the duo, working his way up from features editor at the Purdue student newspaper to the *Indianapolis Star* and Gannett before landing at the Post in 2010.

Today, Prakash and Marburger are the newspaper's digital killers. They talk more to Bezos than anyone else in the newsroom, including Baron. That makes them critical to the continued success of the *Post*, but also important players in the future of newspapers, as owners and editors around the world increasingly look to the *Post* as a turnaround that is working (albeit one made easier by what must seem to competitors like a bottomless Bezos checkbook).

Prakash and Marburger talked to CJR Editor and Publisher Kyle Pope in the Post newsroom about their boss, how they convince print reporters and editors to think digitally, and where the newspaper industry now sits on the innovation curve. An edited transcript follows.

CJR: There is a lot of angst in the industry about the business model of newspapers. How do you feel about your progress in solving the question?

Shailesh Prakash: The first thing we all have to accept is that no one has figured it out. If no one has figured it out, then I don't see any other option than to try and experiment.

CJR: In other words, doing things the way they've been done is out of the question.

SP: I think so. So the next question I get asked—and it's a valid question—is how much will this experimentation cost? Can you afford it? Is it just because Bezos is giving you money?

First I think there's a flaw in the [notion] that experimentation means gobs and gobs of money. It doesn't have to.

Let's take a couple of examples. Right now, we are partnering with Google on an ultra-fast mobile site. As of this instant, there's a little less than 10 percent of our traffic that's flowing into it. Now let's say we find that it doesn't work, or it needs a lot of extra work. It's an option to shut it down.

You haven't done the traditional "Let's make a great plan, let's hire the engineers, let's then build it out, then oops, it didn't work."

CJR: Let's just get back to how that relates to the business model question. The issue to be addressed here is that one of the big impediments you have to growing your audience is the time it takes for stories to load. So you improve that through this mobile technology and you get more people to come to your site. But then what?

SP: What will actually come of that is an open question. Will subscribers pay for an extra-fast site? Will ad blockers stop blocking sites that don't have the wait time that they're used to? These things are unknown. But it begins with trying an experiment.

And then there's a little bit of tangential business model. How much will other publishers pay us if we could improve their mobile site not just a little bit, but significantly? Can I sell that technology to them?

CJR: The idea that readers will pay extra for speed is intriguing. You see that as likely?

SP: I think so. It's been proven over and over again that speed matters. In some industries, the correlation is more direct, like in retail. You have a site and you change nothing except it becomes much faster, you see the sales change.

Joey Marburger: If you're used to a lot of other slow mobile sites out there, specifically news, and you come to us and it's significantly faster, you may be more likely to come to us on a regular basis. And you're more likely—which we see already in the data—to consume more content, hit the subscription meter faster, consume more ads, you name it.

CJR: So you think news consumers in the future will make a decision on which Hillary Clinton story to click on based on speed? If they see a number of options and their experience tells them that *The Washington Post* is faster, then they're going to read that one?

SP: Yes. And we see that already. I don't know if it's a conscious choice. I think it's more about not hesitating to click.

CJR: I can't imagine that's a popular view in the newsroom.

JM: Well, it doesn't really change our editorial strategy in any way. Everyone is peppered with links and headlines. But you don't always know what the story's going to be or if it's what you are looking for. But if you try it and it's super-fast, you're more likely to try something else. But if it's more than three seconds or four seconds every time, you're not going to try.

SP: It was Bezos who brought this up. He said that when Amazon made the Kindle, they didn't think, "Let's get rid of the book and come up with a new way to read books." Their whole approach was, "How can we keep everything that's fantastic about a book and also add in the gifts of digital?"

He mentioned that when you read a newspaper, the ease with which you browse it is so much better than digital browsing. He called it cognitive overhead. So a lot of our design choices have been to reduce cognitive overhead. And speed is a big factor. You don't expect that when I open up this newspaper I'm going to wait. It's there. It's beautiful. It's relaxing.

CJR: But what an interesting idea, that this could be important in terms of how young people view news, which is that they view it as stodgy and old-fashioned. And it could have something to do with the time it takes to download?

This brings us to the content management system that you're marketing to other news organizations. Do you see this as one day becoming its own company?

SP: It's a thing we talk about. It's in its infancy. I don't know.

CJR: Is that your ambition for it?

SP: The biggest deterrent for us selling this technology is not that there's no demand. It's not that we're in a crowded marketplace. Most newsrooms have already concluded that there isn't a market leader out there, so they're very open to discussion. The second thing is that I don't have a worry that this tech doesn't work. We've been working on it for five years. We've overhauled *The Washington Post*, gutted it, and done it again. And it runs a 700-person newsroom that's very, very finicky. These guys are on it, they are demanding. Joey sits in the newsroom, he hears from them every day.

When you go and say, "I've got this thing," they say, 'Really? You built it? *The Washington Post*?" If it was Amazon and they said, "We've come up with this publishing platform," would there be so much hesitation?

CJR: Shailesh, you're relatively new to the newspaper industry. There seems to be this love-hate relationship with digital technology and what it's done to this industry. It's offered this enormous opportunity, and it's also offered enormous pain. How open-minded are people when you come to them with something like this?

SP: I've been here five years, and I think I've seen a shift. I don't think we are at a point where everything is enthusiastically embraced right away, even if it makes either intuitive sense or if there's data to prove it. There's often, "Do you really think we need to do that?" So it's there, but there's significantly less friction now than there was.

CJR: Back to the culture issues. Would we even be having this conversation if this company had not been bought by a technology company? Could a newspaper have made these changes organically?
JM: I think some of them, yes, but it would have taken a little bit longer. It's been three years since Jeff bought us. I'd say we'd probably be where we are maybe five to seven years from now. And who knows if we would've done half of what we've gotten

done. But Jeff didn't just reach down to the newsroom and say here's a brand-new culture, here's a bunch of things you should do, here's what Amazon does, so you should copy it. The sheer thought of him spread throughout the company. Over night, we thought there wasn't much we couldn't do. People were a little more accepting of things.

SP: He's also made some very strong changes in the compensation model. The number one criteria that grows our compensation used to be operating income. Did you or did you not hit the operating income target that was agreed upon at the beginning of the year? It was crystal clear whether you got your bonus or not. We were all in it together. When revenue was slowing and operating income is the target, then what do you do? You cut costs. There's no other way out.

When Jeff bought us, within about six months, he threw that out. Now there are three other criteria. It's basically: How fast do you move? It's very subjective. The second one is that there are no sacred cows, to push experimentation. The third thing is debate, but commit. So you can argue all you want, but once we agree, then there's no undermining. Those are the three things that now very subjectively drive the compensation.

CJR: So does profitability factor in at all?

SP: No. It's those three things.

CJR: In my experience, journalists don't care whether you make any money.

SP: I have been in meetings where it is clear that it is not an option for us to simply say, "Okay, this year we need this much money, and this year we need that much." We are working very hard to make sure we are a profitable enterprise. That is very important.

JM: This is still a job, and you still have to hit certain marks. Everything is just framed in a different way. When you have enough people rallied, it's a lot more fun. If you feel like all you are doing is bean counting, then it's not being creative and it's not fun.

So now when I go to a producer or editor or reporter or whoever and say, "Hey, we want to try an experimental thing, we don't really know what this means but we'll give it a shot and see where it goes. Would you be into that?" They're like, "Yes." Before we had to really convince people.

Innovation thrives in companies where design is respected. But design at all levels. There was a time when people would come to me with ideas and I would say no all the time. It was better for me to teach people to be creative than go off and say I'm the only one with all these creative ideas. That doesn't really help.

CJR: The Post is very prolific on Apple News, on Facebook, and you do a lot of partnerships in terms of giving away content. What is your thinking in terms of traffic versus revenue?

JM: We're starting to think well ahead in shifting that a little bit. But we don't want to stop growing audience just to make a quick buck, either. We still have to scale up the audience. I still feel there's a huge land grab on the internet, especially in media. But eventually, you do have to start converting people.

CJR: It's reminiscent of the growth of the Web, a land grab where you get people in. Newspapers are the internet, circa 1999?

SP: In general, that's a correct metaphor. For the *Post* there are some nuances. We had for a very long time a tag line that said "For and About Washington." One of the big changes and explicit changes in strategy has been to go after a national and international audience. One of the things we've tried to do is to look at platforms we might be able to over-index on to get there faster. Take Facebook. One in seven humans visits Facebook every day. It's not possible to grow nationally and internationally if you say, "I will send them 10 articles." If we want to grow nationally and internationally it is really not an option to just ignore that platform.

CJR: So let's talk about the newsroom culture here. I read that Post reporters produce twice the number of online stories with a newsroom of 700 as *New York Times* reporters, which has a newsroom of 1,300. That in itself is a telling fact of the embrace of this. How has that happened?

JM: We hired a lot more digitally savvy reporters over the past three years. They understood that to write for the internet, you had to be a little more prolific.

Also, how we write stories and how we approach them has changed. There may be one news peg for one story, but we'll write it in a hundred different ways. Look at the Hillary Clinton illness story: the video, the combination of videos, the analysis, the tick tock, the narrative. We actually drove the story forward. We're owning more stories digitally than we ever have.

CJR: I've noticed that digital openness, if that's what you want to call it, isn't necessarily correlated to age. How would you very broadly describe who is able to make that switch?

JM: It's the same qualities that make a good journalist, period. They just have to switch the way they think about things a little bit. What if we were printing the paper every hour and your story was going to be on A1? That's happening today. Journalists are smart, passionate, curious people. And if it's applied in the right way to digital news, then it just takes off.

Also, we're really lucky to have one of the best editors in the world in Marty Baron, who believes in digital news and it's all he really talks about.

SP: We also have this tool called Websked, which is now in the newsroom, where basically now for the first time there is a central command where the editors can see what's being worked on across the newsroom—in video and photography and blogs.

You need to input a time to end—when do you think that story you're writing is going to be ready? As your time draws near, the desk will send a reminder: Hey, your story is due in an hour. We see you haven't yet finished the third paragraph. You see the curve every day of how many pieces of content were published by hour.

Marty sets a curve that he wants. He wants 30 percent of it at 9 am. We own the URL America's First Read. We want to move that curve. There is the culture, then there are the tools that enable that culture to flourish.

CJR: You talk a lot about being product-focused. What is the product here? Is it the journalism?

SP: It's part of it, I think. But everything else is as important: the features on the product, can you save a story for later, is it on the platforms, the speed, the crash rate. All of these are parts of the product that ultimately have to go hand in hand with the journalism.

CJR: Journalists traditionally have had a hard time accepting this notion that journalism is a product that isn't just journalism. I think that's a hard shift for people to make.

SP: The penetration and enthusiasm around that concept is palpable at the *Post*. Jeff's a product guy. We talk to him every two weeks. That's what he talks to us about.

CJR: Less than a journalism guy.

SP: Oh yes, he's a product guy. And having that person at the top smooths the transition significantly. People just understand what's expected. It's in the air. It's in the water.

CJR: But I do think that if there wasn't someone like Marty Baron to balance it out, people would freak out.

SP: Absolutely. I 100-percent agree. And there are examples in the industry of that pure Silicon Valley approach. Jam too much medicine in and the patient will die.

Corporations Value a Free Press, Too

Dan Kennedy

Dan Kennedy is a professor of journalism at Northeastern University and has been published in the Washington Post, *the* Boston Globe, *Nieman Lab, Nieman Reports, and Poynter Online.*

T he nation's capital was still digging out from the two feet of snow that had fallen the previous weekend. But inside the gleaming new headquarters of *The Washington Post*, a celebration was under way.

Among the speakers that day—Thursday, January 28, 2016—was Jason Rezaian, the *Post* reporter who had just been released by the Iranian government. "For much of the eighteen months I was in prison, my Iranian interrogators told me that *The Washington Post* did not exist. That no one knew of my plight. And that the United States government would not lift a finger for my release," said Rezaian, pausing occasionally to keep his emotions in check. "Today I'm here in this room with the very people who proved the Iranians wrong in so many ways."

Also speaking were publisher Frederick Ryan, executive editor Martin Baron, Secretary of State John Kerry, and the region's top elected officials. But they were just the opening act. The main event was a short speech by the host of the party: Jeffrey Preston Bezos, founder and chief executive of the retail and technology behemoth Amazon, digital visionary, and, since October 1, 2013, owner of *The Washington Post*.

It was Bezos who had purchased the storied newspaper from the heirs of Eugene Meyer and Katharine Graham for the bargain-basement price of $250 million. It was Bezos who had opened his checkbook so that the *Post* could reverse years of shrinkage in its reportorial ranks and journalistic ambitions. It was Bezos who had moved the *Post* from its hulking facility on 15th Street to its bright and shiny offices on K Street, overlooking Franklin Square. And it was Bezos who had flown Jason Rezaian and his family home from Germany on his private jet. Now it was time for Bezos—a largely unseen, unheard presence at the *Post* except among the paper's top executives—to step to the podium.

Like Fred Ryan and Marty Baron, Bezos was wearing a lapel pin that announced "#JasonIsFree," the Twitter hashtag that had replaced "#FreeJason" upon Rezaian's release. "We couldn't have a better guest of honor for our grand opening, Jason, because the fact that you're our guest of honor means you're here. So thank you," Bezos began. Next he praised Secretary Kerry.

And then he turned his attention to the *Post*, combining boilerplate ("I am a huge fan of leaning into the future"), praise ("I'm incredibly proud of this team here at the *Post*"), and humility ("I'm still a newbie, and I'm learning"). For a speech that lasted just a little more than seven minutes, it was a bravura performance.

He called himself "a fan of nostalgia," but added, "It's a little risky to let nostalgia transition into glamorizing the past." He invoked tradition. Marty Baron, in his remarks, had referred to the *Post*'s "soul," and Bezos picked up on that. "Important institutions like the Post have an essence, they have a heart, they have a core— what Marty called a soul," he said. "And if you wanted that to change, you'd be crazy. That's part of what this place is, it's part of what makes it so special."

And, finally, he offered some humor aimed at charging up the troops: "Even in the world of journalism, I think the *Post* is just a little more swashbuckling. There's a little more swagger. There's a tiny bit of *bad-assness* here at the *Post*." Bezos paused while the audience laughed and applauded, then continued: "And that is pretty special. Without quality journalism, swashbuckling would just be dumb. Swashbuckling without professionalism leads to those epic-fail YouTube videos. It's the quality journalism at the heart of everything. And then when you add that swagger and that swashbuckling, that's making this place very, very special."

The vision Bezos outlined for his newspaper that day was simultaneously inspiring and entirely at odds with the wretched state of the news business. Of course, the *Post* is different—but in large measure because of Bezos's vast personal wealth (his stake in Amazon was worth an estimated $46 billion in early 2016) and his willingness to spend some of it on his newspaper. Inside the *Post*, all was optimism and hope. Elsewhere, it was cold and bitter. At a time when virtually every newspaper's staff was being cut in an effort to stay ahead of diminishing revenues, the *Post* was moving in an entirely different direction.

Insiders at the *Post* emphasize that Bezos is operating the *Post* as a business, not as an extravagant personal plaything. Although he has bolstered the newsroom, its staffing remains well below the level it reached at the peak of the Graham era. But almost alone among owners of major newspapers, he has shown a willingness to invest now in the hopes of reaching future profitability.

The Washington Post's revival under Jeff Bezos is not just the story of one newspaper. Of far more significance is what it might tell us about prospects for the newspaper business as a whole. Because the internet has led to profound changes in the way journalism is distributed and paid for (or not paid for), newspapers have been struggling since the mid–1990s, slowly at first and more rapidly during the past decade. The purpose of this paper is to analyze what steps Bezos and his team are taking to restore the *Post* not just to its former status as a powerhouse news organization with the resources to compete as a leading source of national and international news, but also to achieve some measure of profitability—and perhaps to serve as a lesson for newspaper owners everywhere.

As we will see, Bezos's *Post* has invested an enormous effort in building the paper's digital audience, now the largest among American newspapers. In 2014 Matthew Hindman, a professor of media and public affairs at George Washington University, identified a number of steps that newspapers should take to increase online traffic. Significantly, the *Post* has taken every one of them: it has boosted the speed of its website and of its various mobile apps; it has lavished attention on the design and layout of those digital platforms; it is developing personalized recommendation systems; it is publishing more content with frequent updates; it regularly tests different headlines and story treatments to see which attract more readers; it is fully engaged with social media; and it offers a considerable amount of multimedia content, with a heavy emphasis on video.

The strategies Bezos is pursuing are applicable to any newspaper: invest in journalism and technology, understanding that a news organization's consumers will not pay more for less; pursue both large-scale and elite audiences, a strategy that could be called mass and class; and maintain a relentless focus on building the size of the digital audience. The specifics of how the *Post* is dealing with those challenges will be discussed later in this paper.

Bezos, who rarely speaks to journalists (even reporters at the *Post*), was not interviewed for this paper. He did not respond to a number of requests sent by email and regular mail over a period of months to him and to several public-relations executives at both Amazon and the *Post*. But in his remarks at the dedication, he said he bought the *Post* because of its importance as an institution—and he emphasized that transforming it into a profitable enterprise will make it stronger journalistically as well.

"The people who meet with me here at the *Post* will have heard me many times say we're not a snack-food company. What we're doing here is really important. It's different," he said. "This needs to be a sustainable business because that's healthy for the mission. But that's not why we do this business. We're not just trying to make money. We think this is important."

A Breathtaking Decline

The disintegration of the news business—and, especially, of newspapers, which continue to produce most of the journalism aimed at holding government and other powerful institutions to account—has been nothing short of breathtaking. Paid daily circulation in the United States fell from a post–1940 high of more than 60 million in 1968 to just 40.4 million in 2014, with a similarly calamitous decline on Sundays. Advertising revenue plunged from $49.4 billion in 2005 to just $19.9 billion in 2014; even worse, the digital share of that total, $3.5 billion in 2014, had barely budged since 2007. Full-time newsroom employment fell from 56,900 in 1989 to 36,700 in 2013.

Thus no small amount of hopeful longing greeted Bezos's acquisition of the *Post* in 2013. Two other wealthy newspaper owners also gave rise to some cautious optimism that year—Aaron Kushner, a former greeting-card executive who was rebuilding *The Orange County Register*, and Boston Red Sox owner John Henry, a wealthy financier who purchased *The Boston Globe* just three days before Bezos made his move. By the spring of 2016, though, Kushner was long gone and Henry was having his ups and downs with the *Globe*. Bezos, on the other hand, was firing on all cylinders.

One of the most significant milestones of the Bezos era came in October 2015, when the *Post* moved ahead of *The New York Times* in web traffic. According to the analytics firm comScore, the *Post* attracted 66.9 million unique visitors that month compared to 65.8 million for the *Times*—a 59 percent increase for the *Post* over the previous year. And the good news continued. In February 2016, according to comScore, the *Post* received 890.1 million page views, beating not just the *Times*(721.3 million) but the traffic monster *BuzzFeed* (884 million) as well, although by some measures *BuzzFeed* continued to be ahead. The only American news site that attracted a larger audience was CNN.com, with more than 1.4 billion page views.

The *Post*'s growth in online readership has been accompanied by a continuing drop in paid print circulation. As is the case with virtually all newspapers, the *Post*'s print edition has shrunk substantially over the years and will almost certainly continue to do so. In September 2015, the Alliance for Audited Media reported that the *Post*'s weekday circulation was about 432,000—just a little more than half of its peak, 832,000, which it reached in 1993. Sunday circulation, meanwhile, slid from 881,000 in 2008 to 572,000 in September 2015. Given the newspaper business's continued reliance on print for most of its revenues, the Graham family clearly would have faced a difficult challenge if the decision hadn't been made to sell the paper.

Indeed, under Graham family ownership, the size of the *Post*'s newsroom had been shrinking for years. Under Bezos, it has been growing. As of March 2016, the *Post* employed about 700 full-time journalists, an expansion of about 140 positions from the time that Bezos bought the paper. That's about half the number employed by *The New York Times*, but it is enough to allow the *Post* to deploy reporters both nationally and internationally to a degree not previously possible. In addition, the *Post* has bolstered the ranks of its engineers by thirty-five positions since Bezos assumed ownership, with eighty engineers working alongside journalists in the newsroom. Those engineers—led by chief information officer and vice president of technology Shailesh Prakash, a highly regarded Graham-era holdover—are involved in an array of projects, from building the paper's website and apps, to designing tools for infographics and database reporting, to developing an in-house content-management system and analytics dashboard.

Then there are the intangibles. Bezos had the good sense to retain not just Prakash but also Marty Baron, who had been hired by Katharine Weymouth, the last of the Graham family publishers. Baron is widely considered to be one of the best editors working today. (A headline in *Esquire* asked, "Is Martin Baron the Best Editor of All Time?") In addition, the *Post* won national attention—and Pulitzer Prizes—for its coverage (along with *The Guardian*) of Edward Snowden's revelations about the National Security Agency, lapses within the Secret Service, and police-involved shootings of civilians. The paper's principled and very public advocacy on Jason Rezaian's behalf served as a reminder of the *Post*'s institutional importance.

Baron speaks of Bezos's approach as one of a willingness to try out a variety of new ideas in the hopes that some of them will work. "He said at the beginning—he was absolutely straightforward about it—that he didn't have a plan in his pocket, he wasn't coming in with the magic pill, the silver bullet, whatever term we want to use," Baron told me. "He wanted to try a lot of different things, most of which have worked pretty well and others that are still to be proven out."

Bezos actually represents *The Washington Post*'s second brush with New Economy wealth. The first came in 2005, when Post Company chief executive Donald Graham graciously allowed Mark Zuckerberg—then the twenty-year-old founder of a tech start-up called Thefacebook—to walk away from a handshake agreement that would have given the Post Company a 10 percent stake in return for a $6 million investment. Zuckerberg accepted a higher offer from Accel, a Silicon Valley–based venture-capital firm. Zuckerberg and Graham remained close, with Graham later serving as a member of Facebook's board. But the opportunity to fund the Post with Facebook riches was lost.

During the final years of Graham ownership, the *Post* got much, much smaller. In 2008, with losses mounting, 231 employees took early-retirement buyouts. Over the previous five years, the size of the newsroom had shrunk from more than 900 full-time journalists to fewer than 700. The Post Company's revenues fell by 10 percent, to $3.15 billion, during the first three quarters of 2011. Profit was down 72 percent, to $55 million. Toward the end, the *Post* itself was losing money, at least on paper: the company's newspaper division (which also included a few smaller publications) reported an operating loss of $9.8 million in 2010, $18.2 million in 2011 (later revised to $21.2 million), and $53.7 million in 2012, according to filings with the Securities and Exchange Commission.

Despite all that, Don Graham, in messages to shareholders and employees, said that the *Post* remained profitable in the years leading up to the sale. In the Washington Post Company's 2012 annual report, Graham wrote that the *Post* had recorded its third straight profitable year "before one-time costs and non-cash pension expense." And in his remarks to *Post* employees on the day that the sale to Bezos was announced, he said that cost-cutting had enabled the *Post* to remain in the black. "As the *Post* fell to tens of millions of dollars in losses in 2009, I wasn't sure the paper could be profitable again soon," Graham said. He praised publisher Katharine Weymouth (his niece) "and her outstanding team" for returning the paper "to cash-flow profitability the next year, and it remains there, making your job and Jeff's far easier."

Indeed, Graham sounded as though his family might be able to keep the *Post* indefinitely when he spoke with interviewers in April 2013. "We are uniquely structured so we didn't give a damn what we made for any given quarter or any year," he said. "That remains the great strength of the place. As a business, the Washington Post Company can be genuinely, no kidding, long-term-minded. If somebody said to me there's a way out for newspapers but you're going to have to lose $100 million a year to get there four to five years from now I would sign up for it in a minute."

Four months later, Graham announced that Jeff Bezos would buy the Post.

On Monday, August 5, staff members gathered in the *Washington Post*'s auditorium for a 4:30 p.m. meeting. As rumor had it, Graham would announce that the paper's building had been sold. The news turned out to be quite a bit more significant than that. In an interview with his own paper, Graham echoed what he had said in April, that the sale was not strictly necessary. Nevertheless, he suggested that continued Graham-family stewardship would have meant a subsistence existence for the *Post*, and he wanted more than that. "The *Post* could have survived under the company's ownership and been profitable for the foreseeable future," Graham said. "But we wanted to do more than survive. I'm not saying this guarantees success, but it gives us a much greater chance of success."

Within a few weeks, Bezos arrived in Washington for two days of meetings to see what he was getting for his $250 million. During a town hall–style meeting with employees, he made it clear that he had thought a great deal about what the *Post* needed to move forward. He promised to support the paper's investigative reporting efforts. And he identified a story that he particularly liked, "9 questions about Syria that you were too embarrassed to ask," which combined substantive background information on that country's conflict, an informal tone, and even a link to a song by a Syrian pop star. It was exactly the kind of serious story with a light approach that has come to define a certain subset of *Post* journalism.

Intriguingly, Bezos also outlined a couple of thoughts that seemed more in keeping with those of a digital troglodyte than with someone who had built one of the world's most successful technology companies. The first were his lamentations over the rise of aggregators such as *The Huffington Post*, which could rewrite a story that had taken journalists months to report "in seventeen minutes," as he put it. The second was his belief in the primacy of the "bundle"—that is, the package of local, national, and international news, sports, culture, business, entertainment, comics, and everything else that comprised the traditional print newspaper. Bezos was not advocating a return to print, of course, though he said it would continue to be an important medium for readers who lived in the Washington area. But he did say that he thought selling a *Washington Post* bundle to subscribers via tablet was a more promising proposition than getting people to pay for one story at a time on the web. "People will buy a package," Bezos said. "They will not pay for a story."

Bezos's latter point brought a retort by one of the *Post*'s own journalists, Timothy B. Lee, who wrote that social sharing through Facebook and Twitter was simply a superior way of being exposed to the best journalism across the web. A new generation of news consumers, Lee said, had no interest in chaining themselves to—and paying for—news from just a few outlets. "Trying to recreate the 'bundle' experience in Web or tablet form means working against the grain of how readers, especially younger readers, consume the news today," Lee wrote. "In the long run, it's a recipe for an aging readership and slow growth."

Lee's warnings notwithstanding, the *Post* has had some success in appealing to younger readers. Citing statistics from comScore, the *Post* reported that it had 56 million mobile users in March 2016, an increase of 61 percent over the previous year. Even more encouraging, 45 percent of the *Post*'s mobile audience were millennials. Mobile usage matters. ComScore found in 2014 that millennials—generally defined as people between the ages of eighteen and thirty-four—are not only more likely to access the internet on their smartphones or tablets than are older generations, but a significant proportion of them use mobile exclusively. That proportion is only going to grow over time.

Essentially, Bezos has taken a multifaceted approach, embracing the bundle that Timothy Lee disparaged as well as social media. And he is offering different versions of that bundle aimed at different types of news consumers.

[…]

Conclusion

In late October 2015, Bob Woodward, the legendary *Washington Post* reporter who was one-half of the duo that brought down a president, spoke at the First Parish Church in Cambridge, Massachusetts, to promote a new book. *The Last of the President's Men* was about Alexander Butterfield, the aide who revealed the existence of the taping system in Richard Nixon's White House, thus proving that he really was a crook. Toward the end of the evening, a member of the audience asked Woodward how the media business had changed over the years. Woodward responded by praising Jeff Bezos.

"I think he's helping us as a business," Woodward said. "It's a better website. I find things much more authoritative, quite frankly, than *The New York Times*." He continued: "Bezos is good news for the newspaper, *The Washington Post*. I think he has a long-range view, staying in for fifteen or twenty years and making sure *The Washington Post* is one of the surviving news sources in the country."

In assessing the Bezos effect, three factors stand out as unique to the *Post* and are thus not replicable elsewhere: the newspaper's location, in Washington, which made the transition from a regional to a national newspaper relatively simple; Bezos's deep pockets, which give him the ability to provide the *Post* with "runway," as he has put it, providing the paper with time and resources to figure out a path to sustainability; and Bezos's position as chief executive of Amazon. Bezos has already made the *Post*'s national digital edition part of Amazon Prime and the Kindle Fire. And as the media analyst Ken Doctor told me, Bezos may see having "a lead dog in the news industry" as a competitive advantage as Amazon goes up against other technology giants such as Facebook, Apple, and Google.

Given those unique characteristics, it is not readily apparent what other newspaper owners could learn from Bezos. Nevertheless, there are a few areas—some specific, some more attitudinal—from which newspapers could in fact benefit by studying the Bezos model. Some of these include:

- **There are significant benefits to private ownership.** Before Bezos bought the *Post*, the Washington Post Company was publicly traded. As with the Sulzberger family at the New York Times Company, the Grahams had set up their governance structure so that the family controlled a majority of the voting stock—thus the Grahams were less beholden to Wall Street's demands for profit than most public companies. Nevertheless, they still had the fiduciary responsibility of trying to maximize profits or at least minimize losses. By contrast, Bezos can invest for the long term.
- **There is value in getting big.** At Amazon, an early imperative was to "Get Big Fast." That has been true at the *Post* as well, even as paid print circulation has continued to decline. By opening the top of the customer-engagement funnel as wide as possible, the *Post* has given itself a larger audience to try

to move to the bottom of the funnel—the point at which increasingly engaged visitors are converted into paying subscribers. In addition, even though the value of digital advertising is declining because of its ubiquity, publishers are able to charge higher rates for large audiences than for small ones.

- **Do not pursue change for change's sake.** Bezos, to his credit, retained Marty Baron as the *Post*'s executive editor and Shailesh Prakash as the chief information officer. Baron is a major asset both internally and externally: he is an outstanding editor whose increasingly high profile has made him an important part of the *Post*'s brand. Prakash's retention was perhaps more surprising given Bezos's technology background. By all accounts he is one of the leading figures in digital news; it speaks well of Bezos's judgment that he did not replace Prakash with someone from Amazon.
- **Technology is central to the mission.** Certainly not every news organization can develop its own technology the way that the *Post* has, and in fact Prakash has a vision of licensing *Post* products to other newspapers—as it is already doing with Arc, a suite of content-management tools the paper developed. As the *Post* continues to pursue a digital growth strategy, the tools that Prakash and his team have developed will be central to that effort.
- **Embrace change even when you can't control it.** The *Post* is publishing all of its content as Facebook Instant Articles and is providing its journalism to Apple News and as part of Google AMP as well. Though using such third-party platforms runs counter to the goal of selling more digital subscriptions and deprives the paper of customer data, *Post* executives believe they have to be where their audience is.

As a technologist himself, Shailesh Prakash has a unique perspective on what Bezos has meant to the *Post*.

"The money has helped us, of course. I wouldn't deny it," he said. "But I don't think that's the main thing Jeff has brought. And

I don't just say that because he's my boss. I truly believe that. Of course he's helped with money. He's helped me hire people, he's helped Marty hire people, and so on. But it's not like it's open-check season where we can do anything we want.

"So what has he really done? I personally think that the biggest thing Jeff has done is to set the right tone for our culture—which is one of experimentation, which is one of encouragement, which is one of 'find the positive surprises and double down.' We believe we have an owner who respects the past but at the same time wants us to be innovative."

As you walk through the *Post's* newsroom, you encounter inspirational quotes from a number of the paper's legendary figures, past and present. One is from Jeff Bezos. It reads, "I strongly believe that missionaries make better products. They care more. For a missionary, it's not just about the business. There has to be a business, and the business has to make sense, but that's not why you do it. You do it because you have something meaningful that motivates you."

Bezos is smart and tough. In considering his stewardship of *The Washington Post*, it's important to maintain a sense of realism. No doubt he wants the *Post* to succeed, but that success has to come on his terms. Ultimately, that means it has to succeed as a profitable business. Still, we should take him at his word that saving a great newspaper is more important to him than turning around the fortunes of "a snack-food company," as he has put it. Bezos is someone who cares about his reputation and who has spoken eloquently about the role of journalism in a democratic society. As he said at the dedication of the new headquarters, "This needs to be a sustainable business because that's healthy for the mission."

No newspaper executive has figured out a way to prosper during the twenty-year era of the commercial internet. As is the case with the *Post*, news organizations need to be willing to experiment, to abandon experiments that aren't working, and to keep embracing new ideas in the hopes that some of them will prove to be not only journalistically sound but an enhancement to the bottom line as well.

Chapter 3

Does Litigation
Hamper a Free Press?

Legal Challenges to a Free Press

Electronic Frontier Foundation

The Electronic Frontier Foundation is a nonprofit digital rights group that works to legally defend individuals and technologies from what it considers abusive legal threats.

Generally, defamation is a false and unprivileged statement of fact that is harmful to someone's reputation, and published "with fault," meaning as a result of negligence or malice. State laws often define defamation in specific ways. Libel is a written defamation; slander is a spoken defamation.

What Are the Elements of a Defamation Claim?

The elements that must be proved to establish defamation are:

1. a publication to one other than the person defamed;
2. a false statement of fact;
3. that is understood as (a) being of and concerning the plaintiff; an (b) tending to harm the reputation of the plaintiff.

If the plaintiff is a public figure, he or she must also prove actual malice.

Is Truth a Defense to Defamation Claims?

Yes. Truth is an absolute defense to a defamation claim. But keep in mind that the truth may be difficult and expensive to prove.

Can My Opinion Be Defamatory?

No—but merely labeling a statement as your "opinion" does not make it so. Courts look at whether a reasonable reader or listener could understand the statement as asserting a statement

"Online Defamation Law," Electronic Frontier Foundation. https://www.eff.org/issues/bloggers/legal/liability/defamation. Licensed under CC BY 3.0 US.

of verifiable fact. (A verifiable fact is one capable of being proven true or false.) This is determined in light of the context of the statement. A few courts have said that statements made in the context of an Internet bulletin board or chat room are highly likely to be opinions or hyperbole, but they do look at the remark in context to see if it's likely to be seen as a true, even if controversial, opinion ("I really hate George Lucas' new movie") rather than an assertion of fact dressed up as an opinion ("It's my opinion that Trinity is the hacker who broke into the IRS database").

What Is a Statement of Verifiable Fact?

A statement of verifiable fact is a statement that conveys a provably false factual assertion, such as someone has committed murder or has cheated on his spouse. To illustrate this point, consider the following excerpt from a court (Vogel v. Felice) considering the alleged defamatory statement that plaintiffs were the top-ranking 'Dumb A**es' on defendant's list of "Top Ten Dumb A**es":

> A statement that the plaintiff is a "Dumb A**," even first among "Dumb A**es," communicates no factual proposition susceptible of proof or refutation. It is true that "dumb" by itself can convey the relatively concrete meaning "lacking in intelligence." Even so, depending on context, it may convey a lack less of objectively assayable mental function than of such imponderable and debatable virtues as judgment or wisdom. Here defendant did not use "dumb" in isolation, but as part of the idiomatic phrase, "dumb a**." When applied to a whole human being, the term "a**" is a general expression of contempt essentially devoid of factual content. Adding the word "dumb" merely converts "contemptible person" to "contemptible fool." Plaintiffs were justifiably insulted by this epithet, but they failed entirely to show how it could be found to convey a provable factual proposition. ... If the meaning conveyed cannot by its nature be proved false, it cannot support a libel claim.

This California case also rejected a claim that the defendant linked the plaintiffs' names to certain web addresses with objectionable addresses (i.e. www.satan.com), noting "merely linking a plaintiff's name to the word "satan" conveys nothing more than the author's opinion that there is something devilish or evil about the plaintiff."

Is There a Difference Between Reporting on Public and Private Figures?

Yes. A private figure claiming defamation—your neighbor, your roommate, the guy who walks his dog by your favorite coffee shop—only has to prove you acted negligently, which is to say that a "reasonable person" would not have published the defamatory statement.

A public figure must show "actual malice"—that you published with either knowledge of falsity or in reckless disregard for the truth. This is a difficult standard for a plaintiff to meet.

Who Is a Public Figure?

A public figure is someone who has actively sought, in a given matter of public interest, to influence the resolution of the matter. In addition to the obvious public figures—a government employee, a senator, a presidential candidate—someone may be a limited-purpose public figure. A limited-purpose public figure is one who (a) voluntarily participates in a discussion about a public controversy, and (b) has access to the media to get his or her own view across. One can also be an involuntary limited-purpose public figure—for example, an air traffic controller on duty at time of fatal crash was held to be an involuntary, limited-purpose public figure, due to his role in a major public occurrence.

Examples of public figures:

- A former city attorney and an attorney for a corporation organized to recall members of city counsel
- A psychologist who conducted "nude marathon" group therapy

- A land developer seeking public approval for housing near a toxic chemical plant
- Members of an activist group who spoke with reporters at public events

Corporations are not always public figures. They are judged by the same standards as individuals.

What Are the Rules About Reporting on a Public Proceeding?

In some states, there are legal privileges protecting fair comments about public proceedings. For example, in California you have a right to make "a fair and true report in, or a communication to, a public journal, of (A) a judicial, (B) legislative, or (C) other public official proceeding, or (D) of anything said in the course thereof, or (E) of a verified charge or complaint made by any person to a public official, upon which complaint a warrant has been issued." This provision has been applied to posting on an online message board, Colt v. Freedom Communications, Inc., and would likely also be applied to blogs. The California privilege also extends to fair and true reports of public meetings, if the publication of the matter complained of was for the public benefit.

What Is a "Fair and True Report"?

A report is "fair and true" if it captures the substance, gist, or sting of the proceeding. The report need not track verbatim the underlying proceeding, but should not deviate so far as to produce a different effect on the reader.

What If I Want to Report on a Public Controversy?

Many jurisdictions recognize a "neutral reportage" privilege, which protects "accurate and disinterested reporting" about potentially libelous accusations arising in public controversies. As one court put it, "The public interest in being fully informed about controversies that often rage around sensitive issues demands that the press be afforded the freedom to report such charges without assuming responsibility for them."

If I Write Something Defamatory, Will a Retraction Help?

Some jurisdictions have retraction statutes that provide protection from defamation lawsuits if the publisher retracts the allegedly defamatory statement. For example, in California, a plaintiff who fails to demand a retraction of a statement made in a newspaper or radio or television broadcast, or who demands and receives a retraction, is limited to getting "special damages"—the specific monetary losses caused by the libelous speech. While few courts have addressed retraction statutes with regard to online publications, a Georgia court denied punitive damages based on the plaintiff's failure to request a retraction for something posted on an Internet bulletin board. (See Mathis v. Cannon.)

If you get a reasonable retraction request, it may help you to comply. The retraction must be "substantially as conspicuous" as the original alleged defamation.

What If I Change the Person's Name?

To state a defamation claim, the person claiming defamation need not be mentioned by name—the plaintiff only needs to be reasonably identifiable. So if you defame the "government executive who makes his home at 1600 Pennsylvania Avenue," it is still reasonably identifiable as the president.

Do Blogs Have the Same Constitutional Protections as Mainstream Media?

Yes. The US Supreme Court has said that "in the context of defamation law, the rights of the institutional media are no greater and no less than those enjoyed by other individuals and organizations engaged in the same activities."

What If I Republish Another Person's Statement? (i.e. Someone Comments on Your Posts)

Generally, anyone who repeats someone else's statements is just as responsible for their defamatory content as the original speaker—if they knew, or had reason to know, of the defamation. Recognizing the difficulty this would pose in the online world, Congress enacted Section 230 of the Communications Decency Act, which provides a strong protection against liability for Internet "intermediaries" who provide or republish speech by others.

The vast weight of authority has held that Section 230 precludes liability for an intermediary's distribution of defamation. While one California court had held that the federal law does not apply to an online distributor's liability in a defamation case, the case, Barrett v. Rosenthal, was overturned by the California Supreme Court (EFF filed an amicus brief in this case).

Can I Get Insurance to Cover Defamation Claims?

Yes. Many insurance companies are now offering media liability insurance policies designed to cover online libel claims. However, the costs could be steep for small blogs—The minimum annual premium is generally $2,500 for a $1 million limit, with a minimum deductible of $5,000. In addition, the insurer will conduct a review of the publisher, and may insist upon certain standards and qualifications (i.e. procedures to screen inflammatory/offensive content, procedures to "take down" content after complaint). The Online Journalism Review has an extensive guide to libel insurance for online publishers.

Will My Homeowner's or Renter's Insurance Policy Cover Libel Lawsuits?

Maybe. Eugene Volokh's the Volokh Conspiracy notes that homeowner's insurance policies, and possibly also some renter's or umbrella insurance policies, generally cover libel lawsuits, though they usually exclude punitive damages and liability related to "business pursuits." (This would generally exclude blogs with any advertising.) You should read your insurance policy carefully to see what coverage it may provide.

What's the Statute of Limitation on Libel?

Most states have a statute of limitations on libel claims, after which point the plaintiff cannot sue over the statement. For example, in California, the one-year statute of limitations starts when the statement is first published to the public. In certain circumstances, such as when the defendant cannot be identified, a plaintiff can have more time to file a claim. Most courts have rejected claims that publishing online amounts to "continuous" publication, and start the statute of limitations ticking when the claimed defamation was first published.

What Are Some Examples of Libelous and Non-Libelous Statements?

The following are a couple of examples from California cases; note the law may vary from state to state. Libelous (when false):

- Charging someone with being a communist (in 1959)
- Calling an attorney a "crook"
- Describing a woman as a call girl
- Accusing a minister of unethical conduct
- Accusing a father of violating the confidence of son

Not-libelous:

- Calling a political foe a "thief" and "liar" in chance encounter (because hyperbole in context)
- Calling a TV show participant a "local loser," "chicken butt" and "big skank"
- Calling someone a "b**ch" or a "son of a b**ch"
- Changing product code name from "Carl Sagan" to "Butt Head Astronomer"

Since libel is considered in context, do not take these examples to be a hard and fast rule about particular phrases. Generally, the non-libelous examples are hyperbole or opinion, while the libelous statements are stating a defamatory fact.

How Do Courts Look at the Context of a Statement?

For a blog, a court would likely start with the general tenor, setting, and format of the blog, as well as the context of the links through which the user accessed the particular entry. Next the court would look at the specific context and content of the blog entry, analyzing the extent of figurative or hyperbolic language used and the reasonable expectations of the blog's audience.

Context is critical. For example, it was not libel for ESPN to caption a photo "Evel Knievel proves you're never too old to be a pimp," since it was (in context) "not intended as a criminal accusation, nor was it reasonably susceptible to such a literal interpretation. Ironically, it was most likely intended as a compliment." However, it would be defamatory to falsely assert "our dad's a pimp" or to accuse your dad of "dabbling in the pimptorial arts." (Real case, but the defendant sons succeeded in a truth defense).

What Is "Libel Per Se"?

When libel is clear on its face, without the need for any explanatory matter, it is called libel per se. The following are often found to be libelous per se:

A statement that falsely:

- Charges any person with crime, or with having been indicted, convicted, or punished for crime;
- Imputes in him the present existence of an infectious, contagious, or loathsome disease;
- Tends directly to injure him in respect to his office, profession, trade or business, either by imputing to him general disqualification in those respects that the office or other occupation peculiarly requires, or by imputing something

with reference to his office, profession, trade, or business that has a natural tendency to lessen its profits;
- Imputes to him impotence or a want of chastity.

Of course, context can still matter. If you respond to a post you don't like by beginning "Jane, you ignorant slut," it may imply a want of chastity on Jane's part. But you have a good chance of convincing a court this was mere hyperbole and pop cultural reference, not a false statement of fact.

What Is a "False Light" Claim?
Some states allow people to sue for damages that arise when others place them in a false light. Information presented in a "false light" is portrayed as factual, but creates a false impression about the plaintiff (i.e., a photograph of plaintiffs in an article about sexual abuse, because it creates the impression that the depicted persons are victims of sexual abuse). False light claims are subject to the constitutional protections discussed above.

What Is Trade Libel?
Trade libel is defamation against the goods or services of a company or business. For example, saying that you found a severed finger in a particular company's chili (if it isn't true).

Libel Laws Encourage Libel Suits

Derek Wilding

Derek Wilding is a professor of media studies and codirector of the Centre for Media Transition at the Faculty of Law, University of Technology Sydney in Australia.

I t's no surprise New South Wales is the state to kick-start a national review of defamation laws.

This state has long been recognised as the hub of reputation litigation in Australia, and this was confirmed in a study we published earlier this year. In looking at cases in the five years since 2013, we found more matters reached a substantive decision in NSW than in all other states combined.

More importantly, these cases are now quite different from the matters considered at the time Australia's uniform defamation scheme commenced in the mid-2000s. Although each state and territory has its own laws, and matters are heard in the courts of each jurisdiction as well as in the federal court of Australia, the legislation across the country is by and large the same. And although NSW has the bulk of litigation action, all jurisdictions face a similar dilemma: the majority of matters now involve digital publication, and some of these publications – social media posts, for example—were unimagined at the time the scheme was implemented.

So it's good to see the start of what will hopefully be a national reform process, with the attorney general of NSW taking his recommendations to a meeting of his counterparts in the other states and territories this week.

The review in NSW started in 2010 but has only just reached the stage of a published report and recommendations. Consultation across the country is now likely to ensure that the law strikes the

"Defamation laws must balance protecting reputations with freedom of expression," by Derek Wilding, Guardian News and Media Limited, June 8, 2018. Reprinted by permission.

right balance in protecting people's reputations while also allowing for freedom of expression. There's a particular need to ensure that journalism is not hampered by laws which prevent legitimate exposure of wrongdoing and critique of decisions and actions, especially by those in public life.

While this "chilling effect" on reporting has long been a criticism of the way some of our laws are drafted, the latest review grapples with a more recent phenomenon: the emergence of defamation actions by individuals against other individuals about comments made on social media and other digital platforms. When we looked at this in our study, we found that public figures only comprised about one fifth of the plaintiffs in defamation cases. Media organisations were the defendants in only about one quarter of cases.

Even so, some decisions awarded substantial damages for Facebook posts, text messages and blog comments. Some of these were serious matters involving accusations of fraud and sexual misconduct, but NSW district court judge Judith Gibson has noted a trend towards smaller, more trivial matters finding their way into court. These might involve comments made in forums that most people would never consider to be "publications" under the law of defamation. Indeed, a number of these matters involve defendants who don't have lawyers representing them in court. Some of the cases even result in judgment entered against the defendant without a full testing of the merits of the claim—individuals who simply made a post on social media sometimes don't even respond to the law suit.

As judge Gibson has also noted, one of the problems with digital publication is that there is effectively no time limit on bringing a defamation action because the law sees it as being republished whenever someone downloads it—even if that's the social media post this ordinary individual made years ago.

So the review conducted by NSW makes some important moves in addressing the kinds of matters that might get to court and the ways in which claims might be put and defences argued.

This in turn might help to knock out some of the many matters that do not make it to court but are the subject of time-consuming correspondence by media organisations and, in some cases, settlements made simply to avoid the costs of full litigation.

The trials of journalists coping with writs and threats over many years have shown that defamation law is a fraught and expensive process. It's also risky for plaintiffs: our study found that while there are some enormous awards of damages for public figures, overall plaintiffs were successful in only around one third of matters – and even then, the damages may be small compared to the costs.

While the current recommendations are the work of only one state, this is a national issue. Let's hope the attorneys general work together to review and modernise defamation legislation. These laws have an important role in protecting reputation but they need amendment to help them address the contemporary environment and to stop them impeding legitimate freedom of expression.

Libel Litigation Can Be a Slippery Slope

Jeffrey A. Tucker

Jeffrey A. Tucker is the former director of content for the Foundation for Economic Education and more recently served as editorial director of the American Institute for Economic Research.

I t is a fact: the United States is one of the best spots in the world for freedom of the press. The courts do not stand ready to persecute people for saying and printing things merely because they annoy people with power. In this way, the US is far ahead of most countries in the world, where libel law is frequently used to quash the freedom to speak.

This is an especially pressing issue in times when anyone with a Twitter account has the power to reach billions. We are all members of the press. We all need the freedoms that only decades ago were mostly used by major media companies.

It wasn't easy to achieve this.

After the founding, we eventually got the First Amendment but this wasn't in the first draft of the Constitution. The Bill of Rights came about through a compromise just to get the thing approved by the states. But even then, press freedom wasn't taken that seriously by the ruling class. Little more than a decade after ratification, the Adams administration shoved through the Alien and Sedition Acts.

These laws, which essentially criminalized libel of a public official, were widely seen as despotic. Many people were accused of crimes for saying something bad about the head of state, just like in the old world that America was founded to leave behind.

The public anger at these laws was so intense that the radical liberal Thomas Jefferson won the 1800 election by campaigning against them. The First Amendment was saved. But the struggle for a consistent defense of the freedom of the press didn't end there. Censorship laws kept coming back, especially in wartime in the 20th century. Woodrow Wilson and FDR both imposed horrible restrictions on speech.

Prevailing Rule

These days, we are mostly safe from such impositions using the excuse of libel. It is almost impossible for any public figure successfully to sue for defamation under any existing libel law. Court precedents have established that the plaintiff has to prove that the writer had "actual malice," fully intending to inflict real harm by deliberately making up false information. That's a very high bar, as legal experts say.

This is not true in Latin America or Europe, where the press faces down government agents regularly, who manipulate libel law in order to crush criticism they don't like.

The 1964 Supreme Court case The New York Times vs. Sullivan established the prevailing rule. By way of background to this case, during the civil rights struggles of the 1950s and early 1960s, many reporters were nervous about reporting on lynchings, police abuse, and various other indignities suffered by black Americans because cities and counties could successfully sue for defamation. The courts would frequently side against the press, which was forced to pay up. Libel litigation was how the segregationist press beat back investigative reporting.

The result was not overt censorship. The practice created what was called a "chilling effect." Writers would refrain from publishing certain claims for fear that someone would get upset, sue, and cause government courts to pillage the property of the media outlet. Rather than take that risk, the press would self-censor: no overt laws were necessary; one only needed the threat of a libel suit to control the information to which people had access.

In the *New York Times* case from 1964, the paper had printed an ad that claimed Martin Luther King, Jr. had been arrested seven times when he had only been arrested four times. The Times printed a retraction, but the head of police in Montgomery, Alabama, was not satisfied. He claimed personal injury to his reputation. The case went to the Supreme Court, which decided that the Times had made a mistake and not spoken out of actual malice, thus rejecting the plaintiff's demand for damages.

Since then, and mostly because the bar for libel cases is so high, the freedom of the press has been mostly guaranteed in law.

The entire idea of a "chilling effect" came about in the context of libel. If you have to face the prospect of a permission-giving institution with coercive power, you will refrain from saying what needs to be said. As John Milton wrote in 1644:

> For to distrust the judgement and the honesty of one who hath but a common repute in learning and never yet offended, as not to count him fit to print his mind without a tutor or examiner, lest he should drop a schism or something of corruption, is the greatest displeasure and indignity to a free and knowing spirit that can be put upon him.

There we have it: it is a matter of human dignity that a person should not be coerced in the printing of an opinion. The US today provides such protections for print, but less so for other media. Even today, many television and radio broadcasts are subjected to forms of censorship.

The printed and digital press has been more-or-less secure, and unusually so.

Eye of the Beholder

An example of how the rule is breached is provided by Victorian England, which had strict laws regarding obscenity. How that was defined was left to the groups who complained loudest. The courts tended to back them. In many cases, the law was invoked against individuals who attempted to publish material about birth control for women. This shocked sensibilities enough that the press was shut down using the excuse that such talk was obscene.

Oddly, in those days, there were no actual laws against advocating for birth control anywhere on the statute books. But the chilling effect was in place due to courts that were friendly to litigants who wanted to stretch the definition of obscenity as far as it would go.

The analogy with libel is clear. Without a clear standard set by the courts, the press is made vulnerable to every manner of lawsuit from any party that imagines itself damaged.

It took half a millennium to arrive at institutions that established a clear wall here: the state may not, regardless of the excuse, interfere with people's right to express a thought. Nor may the courts act on behalf of any private party that claims to have been injured, unless that private party can prove actually malicious intent and real damage.

Today in the US, there is a high wall between the state and the freedom to speak in print (which includes digital publication).

But how thick is this wall? There are always pressures to penetrate it. It is a problem, too, that the law is not well understood by the public, which takes the freedom so much for granted that there is little consciousness of the dangers of a politician who rails against the media for propagating "fake news" (which, like obscenity, obviously exists in the eye of the beholder).

The Trump Challenge

During the campaign and after, Donald Trump has repeatedly threatened to "change libel law" to open up the press to lawsuits.

"I'm going to open up our libel laws so when they write purposely negative and horrible and false articles, we can sue them and win lots of money," Mr. Trump said during the campaign. "We're going to open up those libel laws. So when *The New York Times* writes a hit piece which is a total disgrace or when The Washington Post, which is there for other reasons, writes a hit piece, we can sue them and win money instead of having no chance of winning because they're totally protected."

Obviously such talk directly contradicts prevailing law, which serves as a bulwark of this essential freedom at least. He has gone so far as to found Trump TV, which offers Soviet-like reports such as this one. It is certainly free of anything remotely resembling libel against Trump.

Should Trump prevail in his wishes, a freedom that all of us take for granted—the freedom to criticize government officials on our blogs and social media—would be severely curbed. It would be the 1790s all over again.

Despite the tough talk, there is actually nothing Trump can do to change the Supreme Court's precedent on the matter. He cannot issue an executive order, thank goodness, and he cannot rely on Congress to act with some new censorship law on the order of the Alien and Sedition Acts. We've been there and done that. Obviously, reverting back to old forms would be a disaster for hard-won freedom of the press.

The Freedom Ideal

Now, we might ask the question: how does a truly free society deal with the issue of libel? Should it be the case that the press can just say whatever it wants about a person?

The standard was elucidated by Walter Block. In his view, no one has an enforceable right to a reputation. Words are not themselves aggression and hurt feelings entitle no one to the property of another. In effect, Block would go much further than the Supreme Court and make it absolutely impossible for anyone to sue anyone for libel ever. As he writes in Defending the Undefendable (1976):

> "Now, there is perhaps nothing more repugnant or vicious than libel. We must, therefore, take particular care to defend the free speech rights of libelers, for if they can be protected, the rights of all others—who do not give as much offense—will certainly be more secure. But if the rights of free speech of libelers and slanderers are not protected, the rights of others will be less secure."

But what would be the results in a world in which anyone can say anything he or she wants? Expectations would adjust, same as they have adjusted for "fake news" today. As Block says: "The public would soon learn to digest and evaluate the statements of libelers and slanderers—if the latter were allowed free rein. No longer would a libeler or slanderer have the automatic power to ruin a person's reputation."

In other words, people have to learn that it is not the job of government to stamp a guarantee of truth on the press. Nor it is a government function to weed out information from the media that powerful people do not like.

You don't have to go as far as Block in effectively abolishing the entire concept of libel to see his point. The freedom to speak and write need firm protections in the law, approximating what they are today under since 1964. Civil libertarians should be highly sensitive to any head of state who makes noises along the lines that Trump suggests. It is very recognizable, salient, and very alarming.

We've fought too long and too hard against government encroachments to accept the slightest compromises to the firm principle of the freedom of speech.

With a Free Press Comes Responsibility

Paul Sturges

Paul Sturges is a professor emeritus at Loughborough University in the United Kingdom and has authored more than two hundred articles, reviews, reports, and books dealing with a variety of issues in information science.

[…]

Limitations on freedom of expression are made comparatively explicit in the formal agreements on human rights drawn up by governments. The European Convention on Human Rights (1950), for instance takes the wording of the Universal Declaration almost intact into its Article 10, but adds important further statements specifying a number of those limits.

European Convention on Human Rights, Article 10

1. Everyone has the right to freedom of expression. This right shall include freedom to hold opinions and to receive and impart information and ideas without interference by public authority and regardless of frontiers. This article shall not prevent States from requiring the licensing of broadcasting, television or cinema enterprises.

2. The exercise of these freedoms, since it carries with it duties and responsibilities, may be subject to such formalities, conditions, restrictions or penalties as are prescribed by law and are necessary in a democratic society, in the interests of national security, territorial integrity or public safety, for the prevention of disorder or crime, for the protection of health or morals, for the protection of the reputation or rights of others,

"Limits to freedom of expression?" by Paul Sturges, International Federation of Library Associations and Institutions, 2006. Reprinted by permission.

for preventing the disclosure of information received in confidence, or for maintaining the authority and impartiality of the judiciary.

These are not the only limitations that might be suggested. They do, however, embody the key areas of concern that states cite when imposing limits on the exercise of freedom of expression. It is also worth noting that national security, territorial integrity and public safety are also the chief basis on which those states that particularly fear what their citizens think and say introduce control of expression, despite formally signing up to the international declarations of human rights.

The identification and definition of limitations to freedom of expression is, as implied above, a dangerous business. Done rashly it threatens to undermine the whole structure. Yet it is a fundamental principle expressed in Article 29 of the Universal Declaration that such limitations do exist. They are expressed in terms of "duties to the community" and their scope is constrained in general terms by considerations that include respect for the rights of others.

Universal Declaration of Human Rights, Article 29

1. Everyone has duties to the community in which alone the freedom and full development of his own personality is possible.

2. In the exercise of his rights and freedoms, everyone shall be subject only to such limitations as are determined by law solely for the purpose of securing due recognition for the rights and freedoms of others and of meeting the just requirements of morality, public order and the general welfare of a democratic society.

3. These rights and freedoms may in no case be exercised contrary to the purposes and principles of the United Nations.

[…]

It is clear from recent experience that offence has entered into the list of forms of harm that would need to be taken into the calculation. There has been an increase of cases in which people, usually members of religious groups, protest vehemently that they have suffered offence and that they should be protected from this. Two examples from Britain illustrate the point that this is certainly not confined to the Muslim community. There was a comparatively enormous volume of Christian protests at the TV transmission of *Jerry Springer: The Opera*, in which there was a comic and disrespectful portrayal of Christ. The protests included death threats to the executives who approved the transmission. Street protests by members of the Sikh community in Birmingham at the performance of the play *Behzti* (which had scenes portraying criminal behaviour taking place in a gurdwara) reached such levels that further performances were cancelled because of the risk of harm to people and property. What this shows is that the Danish cartoons affair is not unique in turning attention to the idea that the giving of offence might be considered as a kind of harm in its own right.

A recent attempt to render this coherent is Feinberg (1988)'s offence principle. Recognising that offence can be very deeply felt and that its consequences are potentially extremely damaging (as very directly illustrated by the Danish cartoons protests) Feinberg offers what is effectively a means of modelling offence. The principle suggests that assessment of offence should take into account issues such as the motives of the speaker, the number of people offended, community interests, and the extent to which the material could be avoided. This is, however, after the event. Much the same approach is open to those contemplating making some form of communication that might be considered offensive. Thus individuals with sincerely felt views that they knew would offend some people might still decide that it was necessary to exercise their freedom of expression because their point was too important to keep to themselves. They would need to work out whether they were directing their statements to a minority (which might be vulnerable and sensitive to criticism) or the majority (which might be seen as requiring a shock to its views). They would be encouraged to examine whether what they communicated was likely to damage community interests, perhaps by provoking communal strife or risking destructive public protest. They could also decide what forums or media would most appropriate (for instance, an academic journal read by a few specialists or a popular newspaper read by many). Used in this way, Feinberg's offence principle offers a way to balance the danger of self-censorship against the risk of giving offence. Whilst it is helpful, the problem remains. How can limitations be applied in any given case without damaging the principle of freedom of expression?

Working With Limitations
[...]

Taking the question of media first, a speech made on the street (for instance at Speaker's Corner in London, a traditionally tolerated venue for the expression of all kinds of views) a privately printed pamphlet, a letter to a newspaper, or a personal weblog, is one thing. An article or column in a newspaper, a programme broadcast on radio or TV is another. The latter may possibly represent a journalist's deeply felt personal view, but it also represents the editorial policy, whether *laissez faire* or highly directive, of the owners and editors of the medium concerned. It is not entirely sound to claim that the principle that protected the freedom of the press alongside freedom of speech (as in the US First Amendment) applies just as much to a modern newspaper as it did to the eighteenth century newspaper. There is an enormous contrast between a weekly sheet owned, printed and largely written by one person, and the products of a modern media corporation. Many such corporations have global finance, global reach, power over their salaried journalists, and, crucially, very close relationships with governments. Much of what is published via the global media comes from a position of power akin to that wielded by the rulers of states, and the duties to the community set out in Article 29 of the Universal Declaration apply, if possible, more strongly to those who have power than to those who have little or none.

[…]

However, the case is altered when one considers messages addressed to broader audiences and directed at the beliefs or other distinguishing characteristics of other groups. This would particularly apply to the so-called "hate speech", which is a direct threat to the rights of others. This is because hate speech first of all denies recognition of "the inherent dignity" of all human beings and their "equal and inalienable rights" as set out in the preamble to the Universal Declaration of Human Rights. In the second place it can threaten their more specific rights as set out in the Declaration. Speech or other communication that incites hatred, particularly on grounds of race and religion, and effectively threatens the rights of its victims is a criminal offence in the laws of a number of countries. The availability of law that is capable of offering redress for those who are the victims of derogatory communication that does not fall within legal definitions of hate speech is less obvious. Individuals can use the laws on defamation to contest and seek compensation for statements that damage their reputation. This is a difficult road to take because, amongst other things, it allows the author of an allegedly defamatory statement to attempt to show in court that the statement was justified, with possible further damage to reputation. Nevertheless, many of those who believe they have been defamed do make use of these laws.

There is obviously a logical argument that the concept of defamation should apply to statements that threaten the reputation and dignity of a group of people just as much as to statements made about an individual. It seems to be the case that systems of law generally do not easily accommodate the concept of group defamation. Here the Muslim protesters against the cartoons asked a valid question: if the law does not seem to offer them redress, what is available to them but public demonstration? In turning to this they exercised another human right, that of peaceful assembly.

Universal Declaration of Human Rights, Article 20

1. Everyone has the right to freedom of peaceful assembly and association.
2. No one may be compelled to belong to an association.

Here the important word is "peaceful." Human rights and the laws of nations do not permit riot, the destruction of property, assault on other people and the making of direct threats of violence including murder. The rule of law has at its very heart the specific purpose of protecting the peace of the community by denying personal revenge, duelling, feud and riot as responses to offence, whether that offence is verbal or physical. The law takes to itself the responsibility of dealing with the consequences of offence and in doing so creates a fundamental distinction between advanced and backward societies. Peaceful protest and campaigns to change the law are the only genuine remedies in cases where citizens feel that the law has failed to protect their rights.

[…]

The Right to a Reputation Is a Public Concern

David Engel

David Engel is a practicing lawyer in the UK and a partner at the law firm Addleshaw Goddard.

Jo Glanville of Index on Censorship complains that Britain's libel laws are "a malign force" and "the most significant daily chill on free speech in the UK." I would respectfully disagree.

Freedom of speech is not, whether in the UK or anywhere else, an unfettered right. There are sound philosophical and jurisprudential reasons why that has always been the case, and why it should continue to be the case. Most people would agree that in a democratic society it is not desirable for people to be free, for example, to incite mass murder. Similarly, the right to freedom of speech has always been constrained by other rights, such as the law of copyright (designed to reward and therefore encourage creative effort) and the rights to reputation and to confidentiality.

The European convention on human rights, which Index on Censorship would presumably support, neatly encapsulates this balancing exercise, according the citizens of signatory states a right to freedom of expression (article 10), but only provided that the exercise of such a right does not unnecessarily impact upon a countervailing right to privacy and to reputation (article 8).

Britain's libel laws are the means by which individuals and companies can protect their reputations from being unjustifiably damaged, whether by the media or by the NGOs referred to by Glanville. The key word is unjustifiably. Where the media or a campaigning organisation is justified in trashing a company's or individual's reputation, they are perfectly entitled to do so and there is nothing in Britain's libel laws to prevent them.

"Freedom of speech is not an unfettered right," by David Engel, Guardian News and Media Limited, April 1, 2009. Reprinted by permission.

Glanville says that "the key issue is costs" and that "the use of 'no win no fee' CFAs (conditional fee agreements) has turned libel courts into casinos."

First, and leaving aside the fact that awards of damages in the libel courts have in truth decreased markedly over the last 20 or so years, it is incorrect to assume that CFAs are necessarily "no win, no fee" with a 100% uplift in the event of success.

Libel—and other—lawyers can and do act on a "no win, low fee" basis. The client receives a discount on the standard charging rate if the claim is unsuccessful, but that discount is most unlikely to exceed 50%. In other words, the risk is shared by client and lawyer. Likewise, any uplift in the event of success is calculated, in accordance with Law Society guidelines, to reflect the risk taken on and is highly unlikely to be anywhere near 100%. The stronger the claim (and therefore the lower the risk for the lawyers), the lower the uplift for success.

This is a model that is fair to all parties and strikes a proper and equitable balance between affording access to justice and maintaining any costs uplift at a sensible and proportionate level.

Second, to accuse CFAs of having a "chilling effect" on freedom of speech simply does not reflect the commercial realities. A potential claimant who does not have at least a reasonable case is highly unlikely to be able to persuade any law firm to act on a CFA whether "no win, no fee" or otherwise. In any event, all that most claimants want is an acknowledgement from the newspaper or book publisher in question that they got it wrong and are willing to apologise. If they do so at the outset, the legal costs will be minimal and the claimant is unlikely to press for substantial damages. Nobody will be put out of business.

A claim in libel is not primarily a claim for financial compensation. It is about protecting the claimant's reputation. It is therefore simplistic to seek to compare the level of costs with the amount of damages recovered.

Equally, if the publisher is on strong ground there is no reason why "faced with a lawyer's letter, most publishers have to surrender if they want to stay in business." The costs-shifting principle in English litigation (where the loser must pay most of the winner's legal costs) ensures precisely the opposite. The only reason a publisher would surrender on receipt of a letter of complaint would be if it was likely to lose any legal proceedings that followed. And it would only lose if it should not have published the offending material in the first place.

In addition, most publishers will themselves carry libel insurance to cover precisely this financial exposure. If they choose not to incur the premiums required to maintain such cover, then it is always open to them to take more care about the material they publish.

The media, and other publishers, may not like the fact that CFAs have put ordinary mortals on a more equal financial footing with them in pursuing complaints. But to describe this as a threat to freedom of expression is unreal.

Is Public Funding
Good for a Free Press?

A Case Study in Journalism for the Public Good

The Shorenstein Center

The Shorenstein Center is a Harvard University journalism research center named after Joan Shorenstein, a journalist for the Washington Post *who later produced the* CBS Evening News with Dan Rather.

There has been perhaps no other moment in history so volatile and uncertain—yet full of so much opportunity—for journalism. Newspapers across the country—along with countless jobs—are being eliminated at a high rate. Local news outlets are struggling with falling readership and revenues in an increasingly digital age. And as social media platforms become the primary news sources for an ever-increasing number of Americans, more of them are developing a distrust of the news media. Many politicians are widely discrediting and disparaging news organizations, with President Trump even branding the press "the enemy of the people."

With limited resources and dwindling revenues paralyzing the industry, it's clear that journalism needs financial support now more than ever. What's unclear is how it will survive in our relatively new digital landscape. Fortunately, funding for nonprofit news media has seen a notable uptick in support, oftentimes in the form of new types of grants. While funders have traditionally supported journalism through public media, there are now a growing number of nonprofit news sites that are focusing on a variety of reporting styles, including issue-specific, investigative, accountability, advocacy and more to fill the gaps created by newspaper cutbacks and an ever-more polluted commercial news media.

[…]

"Funding Journalism, Finding Innovation: Success Stories and Ideas for Creative, Sustainable Partnerships," The Shorenstein Center, June 20, 2018. https://shorensteincenter.org/funding-journalism-innovation-case-studies/. Licensed under CC BY-ND 3.0. Copyright © 2019 The Shorenstein Center.

Those of us who invest in a better world understand that we need better information and evidence-based reasoning to conduct our affairs, which is why philanthropy is stepping up to revive quality journalism and reconfigure the news media ecosystem. While core funding has always been imperative, it feels like we've reached a tipping point: The case for funding media and journalism is stronger than ever.

[…]

Case study: Ford Foundation + ACLU of Michigan

In Flint, Michigan, reports of unsafe drinking water were being ignored. The Ford Foundation responded by funding the hiring of an investigative reporter at the ACLU of Michigan—the first time a foundation grant was directed to the hiring of an investigative journalist based at a nonprofit advocacy organization. The result was the uncovering of a national scandal and the political upheaval that ensued.

The calls of distress from the residents of Flint in 2014 about the dangerously elevated lead levels in their tap water were falling on deaf ears. After county officials switched the city's water source to the Flint River, Flint's water was literally poisoning its own people. Bringing discolored tap water to community meetings and posting YouTube videos of their tap water catching on fire, locals were doing everything they could to bring this horrific epidemic to the national spotlight. But time and time again, the largely poor and underrepresented population of Flint found their pleas overlooked. Meanwhile, the American Civil Liberties Union (ACLU) of Michigan, which originally started investigating the state's "emergency manager" law, was stuck with questions about how to bring the political incompetence in Flint to the broader American public. After internal deliberations, executives approached the Ford Foundation with a proposal to hire an investigative reporter, who turned out to be the first funded reporter position at any ACLU chapter. This hiring, in turn, led to a set of revelations that changed lives.

Even though the Flint water crisis is a well-known scandal now, most Americans were unaware of the problem until 2015. The ACLU of Michigan and the Ford Foundation, however, knew the disturbing facts much earlier. The issues began as far back as 2011, when Michigan Gov. Rick Snyder appointed four emergency managers over five years to control Flint's finances. These managers, in turn, were granted broad jurisdiction to modify existing state programs in order to save money, and they had little to no accountability.

In April 2014, in order to save approximately $5 million in two years, Flint started treating water from the Flint River, resulting in toxic tap water. "What we learned is the emergency manager in Flint made reckless decisions simply based on improving their bottom line," said Josh Cinelli, the chief of media relations and manager of strategic communications at the Ford Foundation. "The Pew Research Center brought in doctors to perform tests on the water and raise red flags. But what was still needed was a way to amplify the message so that the mainstream media would pay attention."

Meanwhile, the ACLU of Michigan had tried all of the standard communications efforts to get folks to pay attention. Staffers were working overtime, pitching journalists and trying to get people to visit the city, all to no avail. Racking their brains for an alternative solution, the ACLU came up with an idea.

"The Ford Foundation folks and I were stuck, just going back and forth with each other on how to move forward, and no one was happy," said Kary Moss, the ACLU of Michigan's executive director. "Then it hit me. We needed an investigative reporter." So executives asked the Ford Foundation for direct funding to hire acclaimed reporter Curt Guyette to conduct a broad investigation into Michigan's emergency managers, and Ford program officers agreed immediately. The Ford Foundation decided to initially contribute $500,000 to the project, and in total, it ended up funding the ACLU of Michigan for $2.5 million from 2013-2017.

As soon as he discovered the corruption in Flint, Guyette took a multipronged approach to tackling the issue. He produced a mini-documentary for the ACLU of Michigan on the epidemic, started testing the water himself, and even exposed a leaked memo from a U.S. Environmental Protection Agency official that explained how Michigan's process for lead testing in Flint's water delivered artificially low results. Exposing the problem as a systemic scandal with multiple high-level conspirators all the way up to the governor, Guyette is widely credited as the reporter who broke the story and gave it a national platform. Media commentators such as MSNBC's Rachel Maddow immediately started covering the story on a nightly basis, exponentially expanding the scandal's reach and impact while pressuring lawmakers to act quickly. Americans were outraged by the story, finally forcing change.

The fallout from the scandal was swift and powerful. In October 2015, Gov. Rick Snyder announced that the state and other entities would spend $12 million to reconnect Flint to a safer water supply. In January 2016, President Obama declared a state of emergency in Flint and authorized $5 million in aid. And lawmakers are finally being held accountable for their crimes: In June 2017, involuntary manslaughter charges were brought against five government officials in Flint. Additionally, the work directly resulted in an $87 million settlement with the state of Michigan that will ensure that all lead and galvanized pipes are fully replaced in the city over the next three years.

"I've been doing [journalism] for more than 30 years," Guyette said in a recent interview. "I'm not sure I've ever been involved in anything more important."

So what made this partnership unique?

Typically, journalism grants are made directly to nonprofit investigative outlets such as *Mother Jones* or ProPublica. But in this case, the money went directly to a reporter housed within a nonprofit advocacy organization. The ACLU of Michigan is the only chapter in the country to have an investigative reporter on staff.

"Oftentimes in philanthropy, you get siloes," Cinelli said. "You have a program officer who is working on a specific portfolio but not connected to any other ones, which can be very limiting. In this case, by funding a journalist directly, what was created is an entirely new tool foundations can use in the future. This collaboration created a two-pronged approach—one that promotes quality journalism as well as advocacy journalism."

For its part, the ACLU of Michigan couldn't praise the partnership enough. "With this project, I truly had a funder who was willing to take a risk with me," Moss said. "This effort simply wouldn't have worked without a reporter, and Ford has been so supportive of continuing the funding for similar work."

And the project has paved the way for similar ones. Now other satellite ACLU offices are also trying to hire journalists. Finally, the success with the Flint case has allowed Ford to invest more in journalism-centered projects. "Supporting and defending journalism as an institution has really ramped up in the last year for us," Cinelli said. "We have a new focus on protecting institutions, free speech and freedom of the press. And the beauty of this new model is that we can use it to address other critical social issues, like economic inequality, climate change and mass incarceration. The potential for long-term capacity building is limitless."

[…]

Small Grants Can Revolutionize Journalism

Andrew Dodd

Andrew Dodd is an Australian journalist and Director of the Centre for Advancing Journalism at the University of Melbourne.

There has been perhaps no other moment in history so volatile and uncertain—yet full of so much opportunity—for journalism. Newspapers across the country—along with countless jobs—are being eliminated at a high rate. Local news outlets are struggling with falling readership and revenues in an increasingly digital age. And as social media platforms become the primary news sources for an ever-increasing number of Americans, more of them are developing a distrust of the news media. Many politicians are widely discrediting and disparaging news organizations, with President Trump even branding the press "the enemy of the people."

With limited resources and dwindling revenues paralyzing the industry, it's clear that journalism needs financial support now more than ever. What's unclear is how it will survive in our relatively new digital landscape. Fortunately, funding for nonprofit news media has seen a notable uptick in support, oftentimes in the form of new types of grants. While funders have traditionally supported journalism through public media, there are now a growing number of nonprofit news sites that are focusing on a variety of reporting styles, including issue-specific, investigative, accountability, advocacy and more to fill the gaps created by newspaper cutbacks and an ever-more polluted commercial news media.

[…]

Those of us who invest in a better world understand that we need better information and evidence-based reasoning to conduct our affairs, which is why philanthropy is stepping up to revive quality journalism and reconfigure the news media ecosystem. While core funding has always been imperative, it feels like we've reached a tipping point: The case for funding media and journalism is stronger than ever.

[…]

Case study: Ford Foundation + ACLU of Michigan

In Flint, Michigan, reports of unsafe drinking water were being ignored. The Ford Foundation responded by funding the hiring of an investigative reporter at the ACLU of Michigan—the first time a foundation grant was directed to the hiring of an investigative journalist based at a nonprofit advocacy organization. The result was the uncovering of a national scandal and the political upheaval that ensued.

The calls of distress from the residents of Flint in 2014 about the dangerously elevated lead levels in their tap water were falling on deaf ears. After county officials switched the city's water source to the Flint River, Flint's water was literally poisoning its own people. Bringing discolored tap water to community meetings and posting YouTube videos of their tap water catching on fire, locals were doing everything they could to bring this horrific epidemic to the national spotlight. But time and time again, the largely poor and underrepresented population of Flint found their pleas overlooked. Meanwhile, the American Civil Liberties Union (ACLU) of Michigan, which originally started investigating the state's "emergency manager" law, was stuck with questions about how to bring the political incompetence in Flint to the broader American public. After internal deliberations, executives approached the Ford Foundation with a proposal to hire an investigative reporter, who turned out to be the first funded reporter position at any ACLU chapter. This hiring, in turn, led to a set of revelations that changed lives.

Even though the Flint water crisis is a well-known scandal now, most Americans were unaware of the problem until 2015.

The ACLU of Michigan and the Ford Foundation, however, knew the disturbing facts much earlier. The issues began as far back as 2011, when Michigan Gov. Rick Snyder appointed four emergency managers over five years to control Flint's finances. These managers, in turn, were granted broad jurisdiction to modify existing state programs in order to save money, and they had little to no accountability.

In April 2014, in order to save approximately $5 million in two years, Flint started treating water from the Flint River, resulting in toxic tap water. "What we learned is the emergency manager in Flint made reckless decisions simply based on improving their bottom line," said Josh Cinelli, the chief of media relations and manager of strategic communications at the Ford Foundation. "The Pew Research Center brought in doctors to perform tests on the water and raise red flags. But what was still needed was a way to amplify the message so that the mainstream media would pay attention."

Meanwhile, the ACLU of Michigan had tried all of the standard communications efforts to get folks to pay attention. Staffers were working overtime, pitching journalists and trying to get people to visit the city, all to no avail. Racking their brains for an alternative solution, the ACLU came up with an idea.

"The Ford Foundation folks and I were stuck, just going back and forth with each other on how to move forward, and no one was happy," said Kary Moss, the ACLU of Michigan's executive director. "Then it hit me. We needed an investigative reporter." So executives asked the Ford Foundation for direct funding to hire acclaimed reporter Curt Guyette to conduct a broad investigation into Michigan's emergency managers, and Ford program officers agreed immediately. The Ford Foundation decided to initially contribute $500,000 to the project, and in total, it ended up funding the ACLU of Michigan for $2.5 million from 2013-2017.

As soon as he discovered the corruption in Flint, Guyette took a multipronged approach to tackling the issue. He produced a mini-documentary for the ACLU of Michigan on the epidemic, started testing the water himself, and even exposed a leaked memo from a U.S. Environmental Protection Agency official that explained how Michigan's process for lead testing in Flint's water delivered artificially low results. Exposing the problem as a systemic scandal with multiple high-level conspirators all the way up to the governor, Guyette is widely credited as the reporter who broke the story and gave it a national platform. Media commentators such as MSNBC's Rachel Maddow immediately started covering the story on a nightly basis, exponentially expanding the scandal's reach and impact while pressuring lawmakers to act quickly. Americans were outraged by the story, finally forcing change.

The fallout from the scandal was swift and powerful. In October 2015, Gov. Rick Snyder announced that the state and other entities would spend $12 million to reconnect Flint to a safer water supply. In January 2016, President Obama declared a state of emergency in Flint and authorized $5 million in aid. And lawmakers are finally being held accountable for their crimes: In June 2017, involuntary manslaughter charges were brought against five government officials in Flint. Additionally, the work directly resulted in an $87 million settlement with the state of Michigan that will ensure that all lead and galvanized pipes are fully replaced in the city over the next three years.

"I've been doing [journalism] for more than 30 years," Guyette said in a recent interview. "I'm not sure I've ever been involved in anything more important."

So what made this partnership unique?

Typically, journalism grants are made directly to nonprofit investigative outlets such as *Mother Jones* or ProPublica. But in this case, the money went directly to a reporter housed within a nonprofit advocacy organization. The ACLU of Michigan is the only chapter in the country to have an investigative reporter on staff.

"Oftentimes in philanthropy, you get siloes," Cinelli said. "You have a program officer who is working on a specific portfolio but not connected to any other ones, which can be very limiting. In this case, by funding a journalist directly, what was created is an entirely new tool foundations can use in the future. This collaboration created a two-pronged approach—one that promotes quality journalism as well as advocacy journalism."

For its part, the ACLU of Michigan couldn't praise the partnership enough. "With this project, I truly had a funder who was willing to take a risk with me," Moss said. "This effort simply wouldn't have worked without a reporter, and Ford has been so supportive of continuing the funding for similar work."

And the project has paved the way for similar ones. Now other satellite ACLU offices are also trying to hire journalists. Finally, the success with the Flint case has allowed Ford to invest more in journalism-centered projects. "Supporting and defending journalism as an institution has really ramped up in the last year for us," Cinelli said. "We have a new focus on protecting institutions, free speech and freedom of the press. And the beauty of this new model is that we can use it to address other critical social issues, like economic inequality, climate change and mass incarceration. The potential for long-term capacity building is limitless."

[...]

Nonprofit Journalism Is a Viable Alternative to Ad-Supported Reporting

Ilma Ibrisevic

Ilma Ibrisevic is a writer and the cofounder of Soul Spring, a group that aspires to change the way people see themselves, others, and the world.

For most of the last century, news media operated on a simple premise: building a readership by providing content and then selling the attention of that audience to advertisers.

In the past two decades, newspapers, magazines, radio and TV, all had to adapt to a blossoming of an array of outlets on the web, many of them simply collecting and then disseminating news.

The traditional advertising-heavy funding model for media has been steadily plummeting for years, and it continues to do so.

So nowadays, even those online news outlets have to start rethinking their business models.

In the wake of this, other types of funding models have started emerging. Namely, a number of news organizations have started registering as nonprofits. And foundations and individual philanthropists are donating to nonprofit media more than ever.

For example, The Center for Public Integrity—and its International Consortium of Investigative Journalists (which has become an independent nonprofit news organization since February 2017)—saw a 70 percent rise in individual donations over that month compared to the same period in 2015.

What Exactly Is Nonprofit Journalism?

Nonprofit news organizations tend to be investigative and analysis-focused, rather than concentrated on breaking news. These days, nonprofit news covers many types of journalism, characterized by

"Nonprofit Journalism: Funding, Surviving, and Thriving", by Ilma Ibrisevic, Donorbox Nonprofit Blog, January 20, 2019. Reprinted by permission.

original, expert reporting and a mission to serve the society in a positive way.

The nonprofit designation is primarily a legal framework and a business structure. Under the IRS section 501(c)(3)-501(c)(9), a qualifying organization must invest any surplus revenue back into the organization, rather than paying dividends to shareholders.

Nonprofit news organizations focus on topics of public interest. About two-thirds cover government and the environment. Well over half cover education or social justice and inequality.

Many nonprofit media organizations are decades-old. Venerable nonprofit magazines include Harper's (f. 1850), American Prospect (f. 1990), Consumer Reports (f. 1936), and New Criterion (f. 1982). However, it was only in the 2000s – in response to the financial crisis that newspapers faced—that a number of digital news nonprofits emerged.

Since then, the number of nonprofit news organizations has been increasing every year.

Institute for Nonprofit News (nine years old itself) boasts 180 members. INN says there are about 200 nonprofit newsrooms in the U.S. in total. The nonprofit news sector now pulls in almost $350 million in total annual revenue.

While some criticize nonprofit journalism as being 'elitist' or written to be understood only by those who already read the news, others praise nonprofit news organizations as benchmarks of high-quality journalism. Those who praise nonprofit news organizations believe that they satisfy a burning need for accurate information and analyses of complex issues.

So, What About the Funding?

Like most, if not all, nonprofits, nonprofit news organizations tend to rely on charitable giving—primarily grants and donations.

Private foundations are an important source of funding for many news outlets. Foundation funding is a particularly significant stream of income for non-profit news organizations. In the US, for example, 60% of non-profit news outlets derive at least half their budget from foundations.

However, it is important to note that foundation funding seems to benefit mostly a handful of big nonprofit news organizations.

The vast majority of the $469.5 million that 60 digital nonprofit news media websites raised between 2009 and 2015 supported the 20 biggest outlets ad the 20 smallest eked by on just $8.6 million.

-Institute for Nonprofit News

The researchers also discovered that foundation funding has been subject to geographic differences. Twenty-five public media stations and content producers accounted for 70 percent of all funding. Grant money went primarily to stations or content producers based in 10 states.

This means that nonprofit media organizations across the great majority of states lack the funding necessary to fill gaps in newspaper coverage.

This is why a lot of nonprofit news organizations are working on diversifying their income. To become less dependent on foundations and big philanthropies, many nonprofit news organizations are working on developing membership programs. These mimic the subscription models of The Washington Post and the like. They also increase the number of individual donations.

Efforts to diversify revenue streams, a key indicator of financial stability, are evident: More than half nonprofit news organizations have three or more revenue streams, and one-third have four or more.

Even with all of those efforts in place, individual donations of all sizes are still underdeveloped revenue streams for most nonprofit news organizations.

Excluding public media, revenue from membership makes up between one percent to less than a third of nonprofits' revenue. But, the News Revenue Hub recommends setting a goal of 25 percent of total revenue from memberships and individual donations.

A Case Study: Truthout.org

Truthout is a nonprofit news organization dedicated to providing independent reporting and commentary on a diverse range of social justice issues. Since their founding in 2001, they have anchored their work in principles of accuracy, transparency, and independence from the influence of corporate and political forces.

Truthout describes themselves as working to spark action by revealing systemic injustice and providing a platform for progressive and transformative ideas. They do this through in-depth investigative reporting and critical analysis.

They publish articles by both staff reporters and freelance investigative journalists and analysts. These articles cover the most urgent issues of the day: from climate disruption to racial justice, threats to press freedom to campaigns to reform the US criminal legal system, foreign policy to the economy and beyond.

Truthout pride themselves in their budget comprising of donations from readers—and not a single cent from advertising.

As more and more nonprofit news organizations seek to diversify their revenue streams, and specifically to increase the number of individual donations they receive, online fundraising has become increasingly important.

Truthout upgraded their donation process in mid-2017 in order to meet the needs of their readers. They needed a simpler solution to replace the unnecessarily long, complicated, externally-hosted donation form they had been using for years. To process and manage their online donations, they opted for Donorbox.

Almost immediately, they witnessed a dramatic increase in not only one-time donations but also monthly donations. Monthly donations, in particular, are a sure way to sustainability when it comes to nonprofit funding.

Their development strategy is ever-evolving. And Donorbox continues to be a key tool in their efforts to strengthen their sustainable funding streams.

Truthout has raised more than $1.2m and processed more than 45,000 donations using Donorbox's platform.

Donorbox is a powerful fundraising software that is very simple and fast to set up. You can start fundraising for your nonprofit news organization with a fast, optimized donation payment system in

15 minutes. Over 16,000 organizations from 25 countries use the Donorbox fundraising software. Donorbox specifically encourages recurring donations. Organizations can seamlessly embed a custom form to their website or use a popup widget.

Donorbox is free if you get less than $1k in donations in a month. There are no set up costs. If you reach $1k in a month, Donorbox charges a small platform fee of 1.5% for the month's donations. Other donation platforms charge 2-5% or more. This makes Donorbox ideal for nonprofit news organizations.

The checkout process with Donorbox is simple and effective. Donorbox also offers plug-and-play plugins for WordPress, Wix, Weebly, and Squarespace. Donorbox offers a number of other features that can help you revolutionize your fundraising.

Conclusion

Like the rest of the nonprofit sector, nonprofit news organizations aren't in it for the money. They don't have shareholders to satisfy. They're unburdened by the hyper-focus on profit. This is what allows nonprofit news organizations to maintain their editorial and creative independence.

A healthy nonprofit news organization, regardless of its funding model, respects the editorial and creative independence of its grantees. It respects the editorial and creative integrity of content (covers stories on the basis of editorial merit). And, it is transparent about its funding.

Nonprofit news organizations have an astonishing potential. They often use their resources efficiently and achieve remarkable results. Many of them produce high-quality work, even when they're operating on a low budget and are understaffed.

Their work is invaluable—the reporting is fact-based, community-focused, transparent and non-partisan.

Nonprofit news organizations fill a crucial gap in information and knowledge sharing. While the nonprofit investigative journalism sector is still tiny in terms of the number of journalists and budgets when compared to mainstream media, it's gaining grounds.

And in a society where sensationalism and fake news are prevalent, where funding is hard to come by, where the pressure is high and there are information vacuums—nonprofit news organizations are more important than ever.

Government Support Isn't Necessary to Provide Quality Journalism

Bill Wirtz

Bill Wirtz is a Young Voices Advocate with the Foundation for Economic Education. His work has been featured in Newsweek *and* Le Monde.

I n the effort of maintaining "quality journalism," publishers and journalists around the world make the case for press subsidies. In Europe, this phenomenon is largely present, with many papers completely dependent on, or even owned by, the government. But is the state really needed to produce quality content?

Conflicts of Interest

It seems to be a general rule that if you defend a position that also works in the favor of a certain industry, you will be asked who funds you. In fact, this has been so prevalent that instead of debating the actual points, we find ourselves arguing over who has been more influenced by private interests, regardless of people's intentions. The question, however, is never raised for public funding.

With public ownership or subsidization, the stations lose their independence when it comes to critically analyzing a government's policies. Not convinced? Imagine yourself watching a documentary about Silvio Berlusconi on a channel owned by Silvio Berlusconi (which, if you're in Italy, is not that unlikely). Elected officials hold influence over TV channels via their administration or the financing thereof. In Central and Eastern Europe, this is even more apparent. In the Czech Republic, the minister of finance, Andrej Babiš, personally owns two newspapers, a TV station, and the most popular radio station in the country.

Or take the example of media fees in Switzerland: When a group of young and enthusiastic libertarian students organized a ballot initiative to rid the population of a hefty yearly public media tax, public broadcasters, who hold a very large audience, used their airwaves to argue against the initiative. Simultaneously, private newspapers also defended the royalty because of government promises that a part of the tax would be extended to papers in the form of subsidies.

And this is only natural. After all, who would saw off the branch they're sitting on?

Why Have Public Broadcasts at All?

Ironically, the argument for public broadcasters was that they would ensure the independence of media outlets and civilize public discourse. In a way they have—in that private companies are now needed as a counterbalance to the influence of public media. Publicly-owned stations like the *BBC* are rife with controversies. They also offer very high-paying jobs: in France, there was public outrage after the CEO of the state-owned *France Télévisions* was found to make €322,000 a year, with almost two hundred other high-ranking employees cashing in over €120,000 a year at the taxpayers' expense.

In the United States, broadcasters such as *PBS* and *NPR* receive their funding through the Corporation for Public Broadcasting (CPB), which requests and receives appropriations from the federal government of almost half a billion dollars. However, public television receives 40 percent of its funding privately; for public radio, the figure is 60 percent.

PBS and *NPR* actually wouldn't disappear if government funding were cut. They simply would be forced to operate under the same economic pressures as other U.S. media.

A Lack of Trust

The idea that without government-funded journalism there would be no good journalism at all is comparable to the question of funding of the arts. As the French economist Frédéric Bastiat put it:

Socialism, like the ancient ideas from which it springs, confuses the distinction between government and society. As a result of this, every time we object to a thing being done by government, the socialists conclude that we object to its being done at all. [...] It is as if the socialists were to accuse us of not wanting persons to eat because we do not want the state to raise grain.

Bastiat is right when he dismisses the myth that those who oppose government funding of journalism oppose journalism itself, and his reflections should be complemented with an analysis of the unintended consequences of government intervention.

When we deprive citizens of a certain amount of their income in order to fund journalism, how do we know what those people would have spent the money on had they been able to decide for themselves? The creativity of the individual is immeasurable if it is given the opportunity to manifest itself.

Adding to that, it's important to ask: Who is to decide what quality journalism is, anyway? In a way, it should be the consumer, based on his or her need for information. Should it be left up to a roomful of bureaucrats to establish a collective standard of quality information?

Imperfections of the Market

This is not to say that everything is fine and dandy with privately-owned media. Yes, publishers are influenced by advertisers and the need to generate a lot of views and clicks. On the other hand, a new economy is rising, with people willing to pay for premium content or to listen to podcast conversations that last several hours.

It is that diversity of choice that makes the consumer pick winners and losers in the marketplace of media. We should not let the established media tell us that this is the best it can get and that we need public money to sustain it.

If the media landscape changes, then that change should be directed by consumers.

Government-Funded Journalists Can't Hold the Government Accountable

Tim Luckhurst

Tim Luckhurst is a professor of journalism at the University of Kent in the United Kingdom and a former editor of the Scotsman.

S peaking in 1949, the year in which Britain's first Royal Commission on the Press rejected emphatically the notion that newspapers might be improved by state intervention, Sir Winston Churchill said: "A free press is the unsleeping guardian of every other right that free men prize; it is the most dangerous foe of tyranny... Under dictatorship the press is bound to languish... But where free institutions are indigenous to the soil and men have the habit of liberty, the press will continue to be the Fourth Estate, the vigilant guardian of the rights of the ordinary citizen."

That has been the settled view in Britain throughout the democratic era, but as they anticipate Lord Justice Leveson's recommendations for "a new and more effective way of regulating the press," many Britons may feel tempted into sympathy for a substantially less liberal attitude towards newspaper journalism; the one promoted by the Hacked Off Campaign. It has several attributes of a winning cause. Beyond Hugh Grant's Hollywood glamour it boasts the support of entirely innocent victims of malicious journalism.

It would take a hard heart to deny that the murdered schoolgirl Milly Dowler and her father, mother and sister, Bob, Sally and Gemma, were atrociously treated by the News of the World. Only a fool could defend newspaper treatment of Gerry and Kate McCann, whose daughter Madeleine disappeared in 2007, of Christopher Jefferies, Bristol landlord of the murdered Joanna Yeates, and of the singer Charlotte Church.

"Britain's press must remain free," by Tim Luckhurst, Telegraph Media Group, October 24, 2012. Reprinted by permission.

Add to these blameless individuals celebrity hacking targets including Elle Macpherson and JK Rowling and the case for what Hacked Off wants begins to appear unassailable. At least, it does until you think about it. Scrutiny exposes its case as offensive to the principle of free speech.

Hacked Off asserts that a "free and accountable media" can be achieved by "independent regulation of the press backed by law." It is an oxymoron: in what sense can newspapers be independent if they are regulated by statute? Proposals advanced in support of the campaign by the Media Standards Trust confirm that they can't. The MST proposes self-regulation backed by statute and supervised by an independent auditor with statutory authority.

Hacked Off and the MST are determined to blur the distinction between statutory regulation and self-regulation by pretending that they are not really different at all. In attempting this sleight of hand they overlook the conclusions of three Royal Commissions on the Press and the policies of every peacetime government in the era of universal suffrage. Whether Lord Justice Leveson is persuaded by their arguments or not, the Government should not endorse them. Above all, parliamentarians must remember that Leveson has responsibility to advance proposals, but no power to make them law.

Since the emergence of representative democracy in economically liberal nation states, the role of the press has been understood to be one of service to the public sphere. Journalism is more than a commercial activity designed to make profit by selling news. It informs citizens so that they may engage in critical debate about the practices of government and state. It renders potent the sanction of public opinion in order that it may prevent abuse of power.

The news industry is often raucous and impertinent, yet it stands in a quasi-constitutional relationship to government. It informs, investigates and analyses on the public's behalf. Of course, it entertains us, too. If it did not, it could not reach audiences big enough to ensure the delivery of its most important service:

promoting and defending representative democracy while striving to keep it honest.

The price of this precious service has long been clear. Since newspaper journalism holds government to account, government must not regulate newspapers. The constitutional objection is plain: if politicians regulate newspapers, they will make sure they get the press they want, not the press they deserve. This is why that trifling instrument of democracy, the Constitution of the United States, declares, "Government may make no law abridging the freedom of the press." It is why similar reverence for free speech is proclaimed in Article 19 of the Universal Declaration of Human Rights.

Maintaining independence of newspapers from the state is additionally important in Britain because here executive and legislature are not separate. Our ministers sit in the House of Commons and lead a parliamentary majority. This hybrid arrangement gives a British government power to ensure its legislation is passed; a level of executive power absent from other democratic traditions.

To balance it we have developed a system in which additional checks are exercised in the public interest by the courts and the press. Statutory regulation of newspapers would create a constitutional absurdity: government authority over a body the electorate depends upon to scrutinise government.

Zealous supporters of statutory underpinning pretend that this danger is non-existent or worth ignoring. Their more sophisticated sympathisers insist that fears about a statutory backstop to press regulation are exaggerated. Among them is Kenneth Clarke, Minister without Portfolio, who has broken ranks with fellow Conservatives in cabinet to inform "Dear Brian" Leveson that state involvement to secure effective regulation would not necessarily be "Armageddon."

His implication is that opponents of state-sponsored regulation are guilty of wild hyperbole. But I do not forecast an apocalypse, merely a slow, stuttering descent into a version of controlled speech alien to the British tradition. It may take a long time. It may be very humanely directed in the first instance, but the ultimate price of a statutory backstop to regulation of the newspaper industry is censorship. I fear that is what some of Hacked Off's most obdurate supporters may ultimately condone—in the public interest, of course.

But the Leveson Inquiry has made stark one conclusion that is profoundly inconvenient to proponents of regulation backed by statute. Virtually all the behaviour that has provoked demands for it is either actionable or contrary to criminal law. Hacking of telephones and computers, harassment, data theft, forgery, breach of privacy or copyright—these are all covered by existing law. So is contempt of court or Parliament.

Had the Metropolitan Police energetically pursued additional evidence that emerged from the convictions in 2007 for phone hacking of Clive Goodman and Glenn Mulcaire, the moral panic that spawned the Leveson Inquiry would not have taken place. The main failure in the hacking scandal was a failure to impose the law. Had it been imposed, we might have reached a conclusion along the following lines.

There was, in a few national newspapers in the early years of this century, a culture devoid of ethics that regarded law-breaking as a tremendous way to pursue stories. Working with the active or tacit encouragement of their editors, some reporters behaved as though they were above the law. Among them were some whose lack of sympathy for fellow human beings was frankly repulsive.

Appropriate remedies existed in law for all the offences these journalists committed. But the culture of the industry was such that it did nothing to draw their activities to the attention of the police. This policy of culpable myopia reached a nadir when the Press Complaints Commission failed to investigate effectively hacking at the News of the World and compounded its error by issuing ill-judged criticism of *The Guardian* for pursuing a story of luminous importance. Regulation could not have prevented the hacking scandal; this was a criminal not a regulatory matter, but the PCC failed to draw attention to it after the event.

So, no change is not an option. There must be effective regulation of the press. A new self-regulatory system must have powers to investigate wrongdoing and to summon journalists and their editors to give evidence. It must have the power to issue fines for unethical conduct and an absolute duty to inform the police immediately if any evidence of criminality comes into its possession. It might also offer a mediation service capable of handling promptly complaints that might otherwise go to the civil courts. Above all, it must be independent from government, Parliament and state.

My concern is that Lord Justice Leveson may yet be persuaded that such a system can be supported by statute. It cannot. Though crucial, the details of the new regulatory system Britain deserves are less important than this precious constitutional principle. A Leveson Act would give politicians a foot in the door. If they dislike the way the press treats them, they could amend it in future to obtain the press they want. Soldiers call it mission creep.

Reserving such a power to Westminster would make Britain an excuse for enemies of democracy everywhere. Westminster's statutory backing for a Press Ombudsman would become President Putin's State Censorship Committee or Mahmoud Ahmadinejad's Board of Righteousness. An officially regulated press is an appalling idea. A few individuals who have our collective sympathy and who have received or will receive richly deserved compensation might enjoy the spectacle. We would all be losers.

Organizations to Contact

The editors have compiled the following list of organizations concerned with the issues debated in this book. The descriptions are derived from materials provided by the organizations. All have publications or information available for interested readers. This list was compiled on the date of publication of the present volume; the information provided here may change. Be aware that many organizations take several weeks or longer to respond to inquiries, so allow as much time as possible.

Columbia Journalism Review (CJR)

801 Pulitzer Hall
2950 Broadway
New York, NY 10027
phone: (212) 854-1881
email: editors@cjr.org
website: www.cjr.org

The *Columbia Journalism Review* is a journalism newspaper and website that has been published by the Columbia University Graduate School of Journalism since 1961. Run by the current editor in chief at Reuters, *CJR* regularly publishes researched stories on the state of reporting today.

First Amendment Coalition

534 Fourth Street, Suite B
San Rafael, CA 94901
phone: (415) 460-5060
email: fac@firstamendmentcoalition.org
website: www.firstamendmentcoalition.org

The First Amendment Coalition aims to protect and promote freedom of expression and the people's right to knowledge.

The coalition provides free legal consultations for journalists, educational and informational programs, and legislative oversight of bills affecting access to government. The coalition also authors numerous op-eds and holds public events on these issues.

First Amendment Law Clinic

Michigan State University College of Law
648 North Shaw Lane
Law College Building, Room 215
East Lansing, MI 48824-1300
phone: (517) 432-6880
email: firstamendment@law.msu.edu
website: www.law.msu.edu

The First Amendment Law Clinic provides pro bono legal services aimed at student journalists. The clinic also provides assistance for student journalists submitting Freedom of Information Act (FOIA) requests. The group plans to launch the McLellan Free Speech Online Library, which will provide legal answers to often-asked questions about student speech and press rights and will be geared at people between the ages of fourteen and twenty-one.

Free Press

1025 Connecticut Avenue NW, Suite 1110
Washington, DC 20036
phone: (202) 265-1490
email: tkarr@freepress.net
website: www.freepress.net

An advocacy group that identifies as a major supporter of net neutrality, Free Press identifies runaway media consolidation, protects press freedom, and ensures that diverse voices are represented in our media. In that regard, it is a supporter of "media localism," meaning endorsing the idea that small media markets are represented by local journalists. On the group's website, you can add your name to numerous petitions for its causes.

Journalism Education Association

828 Mid-Campus Drive South
105 Kedzie Hall
Manhattan, KS 66506-1505
phone: (866) 532-5532
email: staff@jea.org
website: www.jea.org

The Journalism Education Association is a nonprofit for teachers of journalism. It publishes the quarterly magazine *Communication: Journalism Education Today* and provides a public guideline of standards for journalism educators. The organization trains journalism education mentors who work with journalism teachers around the world, but largely in the United States.

Media Freedom and Information Access Clinic at Yale Law School

Yale Law School
127 Wall Street
New Haven, CT
phone: (203) 432-4992
email: publicaffairs.law@yale.edu.
website: www.law.yale.edu/mfia

The Media Freedom and Information Access Clinic is a law student clinic dedicated to "increasing government transparency, defending the essential work of news gatherers, and protecting freedom of expression." The group provides pro bono representation to news organizations, freelance journalists, academics, and activists. The group has also litigated FOIA cases that have compelled the release of information about the negotiation of the Trans-Pacific Partnership and the rules for closing the military commissions at Guantanamo.

Media Law Resource Center (MLRC)

266 West 37th Street
20th Floor
New York, NY 10018
phone: (212) 337-0200
email: medialaw@medialaw.org
website: www.medialaw.org

A resource for lawyers who represent media organizations, the MLRC Institute's mission is to educate the public about First Amendment rights. The MLRC has most prominently represented journalists hit with libel or privacy suits.

National Freedom of Information Coalition

3208 Weimer Hall
University of Florida, College of Journalism
and Communications
Gainesville, FL 32611-8400
phone: (352) 294-7082
email: nfoic@nfoic.org
website: www.nfoic.org

The National Freedom of Information Coalition has forty-five state affiliates that task themselves with making sure state and local governments, as well as public institutions, have laws, policies, and procedures to ensure the public's access to their records and proceedings. The coalition is dominated by journalists and media lawyers, but their programs aim to help all citizens who seek public information. On their website, you can find sample FOIA requests and a tutorial on how the process of requesting information from government bodies works.

Bibliography

Books

Jill Abramson. *Merchants of Truth*. New York, NY: Penguin Random House, 2018.

Robert A. Caro. *Working*. New York, NY: Knopf, 2019.

Christopher B. Daly. *Covering America: A Narrative History of a Nation's Journalism*. Amherst, MA: University of Massachusetts Press, 2018.

Stephen Gillers. *Journalism Under Fire: Protecting the Future of Investigative Reporting*. New York, NY: Columbia University Press, 2018.

Steve Hill and Paul Bradshaw. *Mobile-First Journalism: Producing News for Social and Interactive Media*. New York: Routledge, 2018.

Alexandra Kitty. *When Journalism Was a Thing*. Alresford, UK: Zero Books, 2018.

Jane Mayer. *Dark Money: The Hidden History of the Billionaires Behind the Rise of the Radical Right*. New York, NY: Doubleday, 2016.

John Pavlik. *Journalism in the Age of Virtual Reality*. New York, NY: Columbia University Press.

Matthew Pressman. *On Press: The Liberal Values That Shaped the News*. Cambridge, MA: Harvard University Press, 2018.

Alan Rusbridger. *The Remaking of Journalism and Why It Matters Now*. New York, NY: Macmillan, 2018.

April Ryan. *Under Fire: Reporting from the Front Lines of the Trump White House*. Kentland, MD: Rowman & Littlefield, 2018.

Charles Seife. *Virtual Unreality: The New Era of Digital Deception*. New York, NY: Penguin Random House, 2014.

Joe Strupp. *Killing Journalism: How Greed, Laziness (and Donald Trump) Are Destroying News, and How We Can Save It*. New York, NY: Willow Street Press, 2018.

Anjan Sundaram. *Bad News: Last Journalists in a Dictatorship*. New York, NY: Knopf, 2016.

Stephen J. A. Ward. *Ethical Journalism in a Populist Age: The Democratically Engaged Journalist*. Kentland, MD: Rowman & Littlefield, 2018.

Periodicals and Internet Sources

Renee DiResta. "Free Speech in the Age of Algorithmic Megaphones," *Wired*, October 12, 2018. https://www.wired.com/story/facebook-domestic-disinformation-algorithmic-megaphones/.

Renee DiResta. "Free Speech Is Not the Same As Free Reach," *Wired*, August 30, 2018. https://www.wired.com/story/free-speech-is-not-the-same-as-free-reach/.

Jacey Fortin and Jonah Engel Bromwich. "Sinclair Made Dozens of Local News Anchors Recite the Same Script," *New York Times,* April 2, 2018. https://www.nytimes.com/2018/04/02/business/media/sinclair-news-anchors-script.html.

Michael Gonchar. "Why Is Freedom of Speech an Important Right? When, if Ever, Can It Be Limited?" *New York Times*, September 12, 2018. https://www.nytimes.com/2018/09/12/learning/why-is-freedom-of-speech-an-important-right-when-if-ever-can-it-be-limited.html.

Jill Lepore. "Does Journalism Have a Future?" *New Yorker*, January 21, 2019. https://www.newyorker.com/magazine/2019/01/28/does-journalism-have-a-future.

Mark Lloyd. "Media Consolidation Is a Threat to Democracy," *Truth Dig.* https://www.truthdig.com/articles/media-consolidation-is-a-threat-to-democracy/.

George Packer. "Why the Press Is Less Free Today," *New Yorker*, November 13, 2014. https://www.newyorker.com/news/daily-comment/press-freedom-new-censorship.

Dan Rather and Elliot Kirschner. "The Free Press Is Under Fire," *Atlantic*, August 16, 2018. https://www.theatlantic.com/ideas/archive/2018/08/why-a-free-press-matters/567676/.

Jim Rutenberg. "Fewer Media Owners, More Media Choices," *New York Times,* December 2, 2002. https://www.nytimes.com/2002/12/02/business/fewer-media-owners-more-media-choices.html.

Charlie Savage. "Julian Assange Charge Raises Fears About Press Freedom," *New York Times*, November 16, 2018. https://www.nytimes.com/2018/11/16/us/politics/julian-assange-indictment.html.

Andrew Ross Sorkin. "Conglomerates Didn't Die. They Look Like Amazon," *New York Times*, June 19, 2017. https://www.nytimes.com/2017/06/19/business/dealbook/amazon-conglomerate.html.

John Wihbey. "How Policy Makers Can Help the News Industry," *Atlantic,* April 1, 2019. https://www.theatlantic.com/ideas/archive/2019/04/policymakers-should-do-more-help-news-industry/586069/.

Index